Testimonials

"All my life I have loved hearing the stories my parents would tell me of their adventures, as kids with their siblings, young adults finding their feet in life and then the magnificent Ballroom days. I always thought it was like a movie or reading a great novel. They seemed to have fun and enjoy life to the fullest—somehow, even though life was tough, it seemed more simple then.

My Mother is an extraordinary woman with a fantastic life story to tell. Fun, mischievous, a love of life so strong that it jumps off the pages at you.

I believe she is one of the greatest Ballroom Dancing women in the history of Australian Ballroom Dancing. A truly brilliant lady dancer, not just on the Australian stage but on the world stage. My Mother has fitted in many lives into the one she is telling us here. I have enjoyed every word, every sentence, every paragraph. This is a fantastic story of a most beautiful life.

Enjoy!"

Donna Shingler

"September 1939, two very memorable events occurred. WW2 was declared and Margaret Reeve was born. Contrary to common belief, the two events were not related. A legend came into this world and the mold was broken. It gives me great pleasure to write a few words about this wonderful and extraordinary lady whom I have the privilege of calling mum.

I would like to congratulate her on writing this book and hope you enjoy reading her memoirs. It has been a wonderful journey listening to her life stories and the lives she has touched. Her sharp wit and incredible humour are second to none. She is a true character who has truly lived. My sister Donna and I are grateful to mum, as she has been a very big influence in the development of our lives and has made and shaped us what we are today. Truly a wonderful mother whom we love to the moon and back."

Adam Reeve

"I feel very honoured to be asked to write a message in honour of the great Australian icon Margaret Reeve. We will always be grateful for the hard work, incredible insight and dedication of Ray and Margaret together with George Weiss, preparing us for our exciting turning point when Greg and I travelled to the UK to further our knowledge and so they say the rest is History!

Congratulations Margaret and Thank You for taking the time to document the past dancing history."

Marion Welsh (nee Alleyne)

"I first really got to know Margaret and her husband Ray, when I moved from Sydney to Wollongong to dance with Kerry Wilson at about 19. Margaret took me into her home and took care of me until I found my `feet'.

Kerry and I were an unlikely couple. I was the Australian Amateur Latin-American Champion and Kerry was number 2 in Ballroom. Although I had learned Ballroom from my parents as a child, I had only competed, at a low level, for a short time. I was not exactly a competitive ballroom dancer. Kerry had never competed in Latin, only done a Gold Medal Test. Margaret and Ray worked their magic with us and, within a few months, we danced our first Australian Amateur Championship, won the Ballroom and came second in the Latin. We later won both styles in Amateur and Professional Championships.

The training and support we received from Margaret and Ray was incalculable, both practically and psychologically. I will be forever grateful and wish Margaret every success with this memoir."

Ann Harding-Trafford

Canada

Dear Margaret,

I want to congratulate you on writing your book about your life.

You and Ray were a big inspiration for countless people also myself when I was Dancing with Rosalyn and Marion.

I will always remember your kindness and hospitality when we came to Thirroul for your lessons.

You and Ray are icons all over the world for your own dancing, training of champions and judging.

Wonderful that your children have followed in your footsteps.

I'm sure this book will be an inspiration to many many people.

Lots of love,

Greg Smith

Australia, World and British Champion

"Ray, Adam, scoot over so Donna's South African friend can sit. You're always welcome up here luv, great view huh, you eaten…? Simple words which convey so much.

Ever since our first meeting on the balcony of the Winter Gardens, I've felt like part of the family. The word synonymous for me regarding the force of nature known as Mrs. Margaret Reeve is NURTURE.

Nurture (verb): To care or protect someone/something whilst they are growing

Help or encourage development

Cherish (a hope, a dream, belief or ambition)

How apt!

She nurtured her beloved Ray, Donna and Adam.

She nurtured all of us, her very large extended family.

She nurtured the principles of behaviour on and off the dance floor.

She nurtured sound, fundamental principles of dance.

She will continue to nurture the future generations her way, her words in her book."

Thank you, Mrs. Reeve.

Bryan Watson

Back to the Ballroom

Margaret Reeve

Published independently in 2023

Text © Margaret Reeve 2023

All rights reserved. No part of this book may be reproduced by any mechanical, photographic, or electronic process, or in the form of a phonographic recording; nor may it be stored in a retrieval system, transmitted or otherwise be copied for public or private use—other than for "fair use" as brief quotations embodied in articles and reviews— without prior written permission of the publisher.

 A catalogue record for this book is available from the National Library of Australia

This book is available in print and eBook formats.

Acknowledgements

We wish to thank the following people:

- The Australian Dancing Times - article by Colin Hilary.
- The Australian Dance Review - article by Peter Smith.
- The Illawarra Mercury Editor -Peter Cullen
- The Illawarra Mercury Journalist - Louise Turk.
- Tribute by Timothy Howson and Joanne Bolton.
- Article by Glen Tierny
- Emails from Makato Seki, Marcus Hilton (MBE) Karen and Henry James Hilton, Marion Welsh and Greg and Jeanny Smith.

All photographs in this book, apart from those mentioned in each chapter. are from the collection belonging to Margaret Reeve. We would like to thank the following people, who with kind permission granted us access to their photos. Alex Schembri, Mark Sullivan, Kim Dorney, Melanie Sears, Shirley Wall, David Smith, Felix Park, Ann Harding-Trafford, Neale Brynes, Ray McMahon and Marion Welsh.

Thank you to dear Maria Timpano for your hard work and patience, in the writing of my book. The last two years with Covid19 have not been easy for me, being in and out of hospital during these past twelve months. You, in your friendship, have come to me every week to encourage and help like you have. I thank you.

Foreword

Who would've thought walking up a set of stairs in suburban Thirroul 55 years ago could set such a rewarding, life shaping direction in a person's life?

Well, it happened to me. At the age of 10 I became a part of the Reeve & Maloney Dance Studio breaking the pattern and lifestyle of a football loving, typically Aussie family, to experience a pastime which changed my life and that of my family.

Dance Studios in those days, were the family that existed outside the traditional family and were the reason for the dizzy heights that existed many years ago in the world of Ballroom Dancing. I was fortunate enough to be a part of the one of the most successful and largest of its kind in Australia. Ray and Margaret Reeve, like many others, created a dance empire from which they created and sculptured the lives of young Australians. Like other dance teachers, Ray and Margaret became proxy parents, advisors and were the equivalent to today's Google, providing guidance, advice and life values in all facets of our young, developing lives. Through the involvement of Dance Studios another dimension was added to competing and everyone, Australia wide, benefited and grew.

How lucky we would be to share the insight and wisdom of our predecessors and this publication. Back to the Ballroom, will provide insight into past successful formulas and perhaps inspire others to share their experiences. The past both simplifies and provides wisdom and direction for the future. Our passion and desire for the growth of dancing could be so enhanced if only the likes of Eileen Kane, George Weiss, Jack Keating, Doreen Costello, Robert Wrightson, Sandy Robertson, Mickey Powell, Bon Gibbons and others had been able to leave in the written form their knowledge, experience and advice from which we could all benefit today.

Back to the Ballroom by Margaret Reeve, is not only a publication for enjoyment but a book of learning for us all.

When Margaret shared her vision of producing this publication I must admit, I experienced some panic. You see our dance teachers in the past knew us "warts and all" however, thankfully, many of these details do not make these pages.

I congratulate Margaret on her foresight and courage to share her experiences. Those of you who know Margaret well would share my view - "if I was in a war I would certainly want Margaret sharing a trench with me, she would fight to the end always having your back." This publication is as much an insight to the past years of Ballroom Dancing in this country as it is to her outstanding qualities as a human.

Good luck with Back to the Ballroom, Margaret. I feel sure your hard work will inspire and delight many, hopefully returning Dance to its previous glory days.

Peter Todd

Let's Begin

Currently, I reside in Wollongong. I moved last year and in fact I live one street away from the studio. It's perfect! Though as time has moved on, and it has, I hadn't realised just how many things change over the years. On one occasion, I went into Wollongong to pay our home insurance - Western Assurance.

Having walked up to the door of the building, I thought the paint work was quite garish for an insurance firm. I knocked on the door and a woman answered. Her response was, "Allo love, what can I do for you?" I replied I wanted to pay for my insurance account. She laughed! "Hasn't been an insurance building for years, but you are most welcome to come in. Usually, my clientele are men and at midnight." I thanked her very much and told her I was mistaken. I learnt later what kind of house it was. No problem!

Since I was a young teenager, I have lived in the greater Wollongong region. Thirroul became my home. As a family, we would frequent the area for holidays and loved the ocean and the mountains equally. Having spent most of my childhood living in Leichhardt, the northern suburbs of the Illawarra, was home away from home. We especially loved the beaches. There are so many fond memories for me.

I began working in Thirroul as a young girl and soon dancing would become a huge part of my life. Before I knew it, I was competing and my life was entwined with dancing. Then I began dancing with Ray and soon we would become husband and wife. Then it was just full steam ahead and nothing seemed to phase me.

As we went through our lives, Thirroul was the place where we would live. It was so beautiful. We built our first and only house together along the lovely green escarpment. In front of our house was the ocean and behind our house was a beautiful reserve and a magnificent mountain. Every suburb along the south coast had its own beach, you could take your pick. Living between the mountains and the sea, the choices were endless.

We became very well acquainted with the locals in the area. Local families who ran and still run their businesses that provide for people every day. I am very well looked after. One of our beautiful families, who owns the `Fruit Barn' has been serving us for years. Their surname is Akary. They are three generations of green grocers. The grandparents came to Australia in 1967 and for the past 50 years they have been looking after our family with our fruits and vegetables - it's just lovely produce!

They would deliver to me every week and they still do. They are a lovely family, so respectful and thoughtful. Jania Akary went to school with Donna - a lovely young lady and she is the second generation. Her son Elie and his wife Sarah have three fantastic, handsome little boys. I bet they will be great soccer players.

Then we have the local pharmacy run by the Smith family. They have lived in the area for years and they are also three generations. They are such a lovely respectful family, who, along with their staff, look after me and nothing is too much trouble. Then there is my Doctor, Professor Ann Ellacot, who has been in Thirroul for many years. I really am surrounded by wonderful people and have access to everything I need.

Donna takes me grocery shopping, to the bank, and running errands every Tuesday and we stop for a coffee when we are finished. I look forward to this lovely time with Donna; she makes me feel so good. I am very proud of her. I feel so comfortable with my life and all my acquaintances in our little *Utopia* of Thirroul.

My life of dancing has introduced me to so many people and many of them became good friends. One of the nicest people I have ever taught over the years was a young lady called Antonella Zucco.

What a dancer! So rhythmical. She and Stefano Olivieri were a very successful couple. They loved their dancing so much, especially Antonella. With Stefano she had a wonderful star-studded career nationally, and they also competed internationally. They had so much support from their parents, especially Mrs. Zucco. As well as her success with Stefano, Antonella also won the Amateur Australasian Latin Championship with Ron Panto, another fine dancer.

A couple of special friends that I must mention are Peter Todd and Mark Sullivan. Peter Todd - What can I say except great friend. Peter had a favourite Foxtrot track called DANKE SCHOEN, released in 1963 by Wayne Newton. He played that piece of music to death! We all used to stir him about it, as we didn't like it, but he loved it. Peter is dependable, good fun and, after everything that has happened, a very loyal human being to me. He and his partner and wife, Debbie, were a very professional team. His contributions to our studio were as a successful teacher, competitor and a great professional in our industry.

It has been a wonderful experience for me and our studio to have reached out to him as a young boy until now. Father of two lovely children and grandfather of 3 lovely boys. To me, a successful and thoughtful human being. We had such good times and still do. He would throw himself into everything he did - one hundred percent, including his career, to helping people in need and the teaching of his New Vogue Champions.

Mrs. Todd, Peter's mother, took in and helped many of our up-and-coming champions, but one of her great boarders who had an awesome sense of humour and that who you couldn't help loving, was Mark Sullivan.

Mark was another great dancer and great friend. I loved the two of them and still do. I think it has been and still is a loyal friendship between the three of us. No more needs to be said. Mark and his wife Debbie had international success. In relation to dancing, Mark's explanation was, "We knew it when it was great." His contribution to psychology, dancing and teaching to this day, is appreciated.

Over the course of my dancing career, people have constantly asked for my advice and/or opinion. I was once asked what I look for when adjudicating? Well, as an adjudicator, to choose the winner in a championship, I would like to see and feel what we all want, the complete package. Usually, we talk about the X factor or CHARISMA. Once again, the formula for the structure of the dance must be adhered to.

I have often watched the final of a championship event where one couple differentiates from the other 5 couples. In relation to that one couple, do they present in their performance the correct technique and rhythmical interpretation? Do they have presence on the floor along with competitive alertness, deportment and inspiring movement? If so, then to me, they should be considered in the running for first place.

A couple who owns these attributes on the floor deserves my vote as the winner. Very demanding and rare for couples to have, although there are the special talented ones who still have the competitive excitement. Therefore, the formula for the structure of the dance is very important. One must believe, love and have discipline.

Sometimes, when two highly talented people dance together, their emotions can run riot if they have a disagreement. Going back to my days, I should have been a cricket player - I had a good aim at my wicket, which was Ray. I always had a good shot with my shoe, right in the middle of his back. It didn't hurt.

After practice, Ray would always ask, "Would you like a cup of coffee, Margaret, or some lunch?" Women live on their emotions and I would always answer very sternly, "No, thank you" and then we would live to practice another day.

We must have had the intelligence and know how to make our career advance and stay together with each other. Ray was a great dancer, a perfectionist, but he did not like to practice! When it came to teaching, we used persistence and tenacity to develop our ideas. I can't stress enough that it is better to have a bad lesson from a good teacher than to have a good lesson from a bad teacher.

When my children went to England, I told them to only learn from someone who can give you the right information. You know the journey. I'll give you the map!

The Rhythm of the Dance

Sometimes, when I am watching a championship, I think to myself, that the only resemblance some couples have of the dance to the music is purely coincidental. If one blocked the music, we could not tell what dance they were doing.

The rhythm content of each dance has its own characterisation. True, the feet step in time with the accentuated beats, but what about the body rhythm, the expression and the selling of the dance and the telling of the story of the dance? The expansion of the rhythm between the beats gives the balance to the musicality of the body rhythm.

We have a basis where to start: with our foot pressure, leg tension and technique. However, far too many dancers, when achieving this to a certain standard, forget the purpose of the melody.

Unlike a singer, a dancer can't voice what he or she feels inside. Therefore, their self-expression must be projected by the manner in which they feel the rhythm through their body and how they execute the dance.

We often say that the champion has something extra, which is invariably described as that certain X factor. Surely what we mean is their interpretation and showmanship of the rhythm and their interpretation of the musicality of the dance.

These things seem to be more prominent on the international scene, even in the lower grades. It is not their ability as dancers but their ability to express and sell their rhythmic interpretation of the movement of the body of that particular dance. I was once told by one of our great exponents of dancing that there is more to being a champion than just being a good dancer.

Couples try to penetrate the rhythm but somehow come up with a somewhat plastic version of the subtlety of the rhythm pulse. Hence the mechanical clone.

These thoughts, of course, are my observations, but I would like to see from our dancers a top priority in the dance's theme and that is the rhythm. Whether it be foot, knee, hip, ribs, arms, face dancing or a rhythmic communication with one's partner - and not to just get up and dance a well-rehearsed routine with the arms or left toenail pointing in a set direction every eight bars. I suppose my thoughts come under the classification of *soul;* which once again goes back to the start of my conversation, coming under the heading of - Rhythm of The Dance.

Margaret Reeve

Contents

Testimonials 1
Acknowledgements 7
Foreword 9
Let's Begin 11
The Rhythm of the Dance 17
Contents 19
My life growing up 21
And then it all started 29
A new partner - Ray and I 35
Ray's family 41
1961 47
1965: The World's and the British 51
New Zealand 63
1968: What a year 71
We were always improving 75
Further learning 79
1972: A year like no other 83
Showtime 93
Celebrities and showbiz 103
Lectures and Campsie 111
The glamour and the friendships 115
Threats 121
Families 127
The Aussie larrikin 135
Hong Kong and Taiwan 141

Tributes	145
Where we got our information from	159
Students and teaching	165
Roll of Honour: Amateur and professional	177
Donna	185
Adam	193
Ray	201
Leaving a legacy	207

My life growing up

On the 3rd September 1939, WWII was declared in Britain. The following day, September 4th, it was announced in Australia. It was also the day that I was born at Nurse Constant's Hospital in Leichhardt, New South Wales.

We lived on Cecily Street. I grew up in a loving household with a strong family bond. We were a family of five - three brothers, Bill, Leo and Kevin, with two sisters Dawn and me. My mother's name was Elsie and my father's name was William (Bill). Funnily enough, Ray's parents had the same names.

Music and singing influenced me a lot and dancing was something that I had always wanted to do. At the age of three years, I sang at my uncle's wedding. The song was `Oh you beautiful doll`.

The Primary School I attended was St Joseph's Catholic at Rozelle, where I received a very good education. Things were certainly a lot different then. I made my first Holy Communion at the age of eight.

Every Saturday morning, I would go up to the local dancing school, which was four doors up from our house in Cecily Street. I would just sit inside the front door and watch. The owner of the dancing school was a nice lady who didn't mind me sitting there. They were doing tap and ballet. I was so engrossed with the dancing. I would watch in awe!

I shared my life with some of Australia's great stage dancers - all from the same area where I grew up. One of my colleagues and OAM recipient for services to ballroom dancing, Neville Boyd, said that this was the home of the tap dancers. Some great dancers in that era were Elaine and Shirley Honeybrook, Patti Roberts, Janice Breen, Edna

Storey and Elaine Gaggin. We weren't wealthy, or rolling in money, but we were all immersed in our passion for the love of dance. These women contributed greatly to tap and ballet as performers, teachers and dance school operators. I would be driven to the ballroom.

Forbes was where my mother grew up and she had some tales to tell. Once she was chased by a huge goanna and to escape, she climbed a tree. Also, on more than one occasion, she and her siblings, the same as I - a sister with three brothers - used to jump into the Lachlan River and take the pump belt off the irrigation system of their Chinese neighbour's farm. They would ask for a watermelon before they would put it back on. This seemed to work as they knew the Chinese farmer couldn't swim.

One year, the floods were pretty bad in Forbes. My grandfather got all the family out of the house. The flood waters were so high, after getting the family to safety, he went back to the house and became trapped. There was one horse left and he managed to free it. He escaped by grabbing onto the horse's tail and the horse swam out with my grandfather holding on.

Every year, our family would travel down to Austinmer on the NSW South Coast for our holidays. We travelled by steam train, which was always so crowded. The boys, Leo and Kevin, would sit on their suitcases on the walkway platforms outside of the carriages. I don't know whether or not it was allowed, but they had tickets. I often wonder how my parents could afford it with five children. They both worked so hard to give us a holiday. Everything was just so enjoyable and simple. The beach, movies, `Chamberlain's Ice Cream Parlour` - it was all so great! The Illawarra has always been a wonderful place for holidays. We would stay at Mrs. Redfern's house, a family friend, for years. Incidentally, her son Jimmy Redfern was a great rugby league player. He was well known and played for Thirroul.

At this time, my brother Bill was still in the army, a corporal in the commando squad in WW2. He, like so many others at that time, lied about his age and so joined the army at seventeen years old. He was wounded, but recovered. Bill's best friend Ray Jones had his leg blown off in battle and Bill carried him for five miles on his back to safety. After the war was over, he was honoured by her majesty Queen Elizabeth. Ray recovered and was Bill's best man at his wedding.

Years later, after I was married with my own family, we would go to Canberra for Gwen Wallace's Dancing Championships. My son Adam always wanted to go visit the War Memorial. As we were walking around the exhibit, we came across a life size photo of my brother Billy, kneeling, receiving Holy Communion before going into battle. As you can imagine, I was very emotional. Apparently, the photo was on the front page of the Sydney Telegraph.

Winter meant football, which was a religion in our household. Every Sunday, we would watch my brothers play CYO football as a family. They later advanced to 1st grade. We would travel by tram, which was conveniently located at the top of our street.

At first, we would go to Birchgrove Oval, then onto Leichhardt Oval and then onto Dulwich Hill - all on the same day. The grounds were so accessible. The tram line ran alongside all the grounds. The cost of watching the games was one shilling each. If you were a high school boy who played for your local club, they gave you a free pass to watch the games.

Billy played first grade for Balmain, then moved to Mascot and played for South Sydney. Speaking of South Sydney, a future student of mine, a young Peter Todd, would come into our Thirroul studio with his shoe bag made of red and green leather, of course. I think he was South Sydney's best ever fan. Leo, my second brother, played for Balmain after coming out of CYO (Catholic Youth Organisation). He was also known as the *Gentle Giant*, just like Steve Roach, who played for Balmain, NSW State of Origin and Australia. Kevin, my third eldest brother, played for the CYO and The

Leichhardt Wanderers. I love seeing Leichhardt oval on the television, home of the Tigers. It brings back great memories of when I was a child, playing on the hill near the scoreboard, which is now known as Wayne Pearce hill. Robbie Farah, another Tiger player, would sit on the scoreboard to show his support and love for his team, The Tigers! I still follow The Tigers and I also follow Sydney FC soccer.

Summer meant picnics. After a 6.15am mass on Sunday mornings, weather permitting, we would leave by taxi from Rozelle church to go to Nielsen Park (Vaucluse) for a day's outing. What a treat it was! My mother prepared all our food, including her homemade mayonnaise. We would swim, have lunch and swim again. Kevin would fish all day. He really was a great fisherman. We would then come home by ferry to Circular Quay and so on. Nielsen Park was also the place where we would watch the Sydney to Hobart yacht race at 1pm on Boxing Day. What a sight!

We often went to swim at Balmain and Drummoyne pools. We were blessed to watch some of Australia's greatest Olympic swimmers in action. Dawn Fraser, Lorraine Crapp, Murray Rose and John and Ilsa Konrads. Their coach had a specific training technique where he would swim his team at White Bay against the tide and the swell, known as The Swifty. It was very fast, hence the name. He would then swim them back with the tide. He was very tough on his swimmers. But what champions he produced! Kevin would go fishing at White Bay, too, and catch blue swimmer crabs. He would get upset and would wish the Swifty to blazes because the swimmers that were training would interfere with his fishing. An art that he learnt was to catch his crabs with horse hair. We also swam and fished at Callan Park.

If we had a free afternoon on Sundays between seasons, my father would take us down to the waterfront at Elkington Park, Balmain, to watch the 18 footers sail out onto the harbour. It was great. The hill of the park was packed with spectators. So much to see and learn.

One of the lovely times of my childhood was after dinner on a Saturday night. Kevin and I would go up to the main road, Darling Street, in Balmain. It was very famous at the time for the Comic Book Exchange shop. The shop was not very far from our house. At the cost of 2p per comic book we would exchange our comics for new ones to read - Captain Marvel, The Phantom, Dick Tracy, Superman and many more. We loved doing this.

The best part was on the way home. The enticing aromas from the best hamburgers in the world would take precedence over everything. The smell was magnificent. It led you straight to the hamburger bar. Apart from my own homemade hamburgers, I have never enjoyed the taste of one like our Saturday night specials in the Rozelle shop. Yet I can't remember the name of the shop. Just the most beautiful smell that enticed us to buy.

On a Saturday morning, if he was free, my father would venture into the city to Eddy Avenue, near Central Railway Station. He would take Kevin with him and they would go to a restaurant called `The Hole in the Wall'. It was not a high-class restaurant, but it was always crowded. The waiters all wore white sandshoes and would literally run to serve their customers. The famous item on the menu was a meat pie with peas. They were fantastic. The atmosphere was electric.

Every Thursday night we would go to the movies, at Hoyts, in Rozelle, as a family. On Saturday afternoons, it was the kids screening. We were given one shilling each - sixpence to get in and sixpence to spend. I had to go with Kevin, who hated having to take his younger sister. He would nearly drag my arm out of its socket. I loved Kevin and especially enjoyed the times later on in life when we would go fishing off the rocks at Austinmer's side beach. I would study while Kevin fished.

Every Friday I would go to Paddy's Markets in Ultimo with my mother. It was a wonderful experience. All the beautiful fruit and vegetables would be on display. My great Uncle who had an orchard in Windsor, would bring his fresh fruit and vegetables to sell at the market. My Uncle would look after our family with his quality produce. Every week I would really look forward to it.

As a family, we all sang - not always in unison. However, we all sang our own songs, usually at birthdays, after weddings or parties at home. Dad's terminology was, "We all had to do an act." So, we did! I think Leo and Kevin thought they were Frankie Laine or Dean Martin, and I thought I was Doris Day. My passion for music now is varied. I love jazz and Ella Fitzgerald, and I love Pavarotti. I don't like heavy metal but I like the group, Queen.

Leo used to learn the Jitterbug at a dance studio in Newtown. His teacher's name was Andy Ellis. Leo would come home from his dance class and show me some steps. I still use those same steps today incorporated in our Jive routines, in our Syllabus.

At twelve years of age and with my mother's help, I made my own clothes. I loved to sew and I would later make my Ballroom Dress as a C Grade dancer. It was tangerine.

My sister Dawn, now 94 years old, is eleven years older than I. She was born in 1928 and is a great person. Dawn was dux of the school, highly intelligent and to this day, she still has a great brain. Dawn always came on our picnics to Neilson Park and yes, she still follows the Balmain Tigers!

When she was in the C.Y.O, they used to have dances in the church hall. I used to love to see her in her - what was called then - "ballerina dress." It was about mid-calf length and made of tulle. In those days, the girls wore lovely dresses to the dances.

The night before Dawn married, Mum told her that there was something she needed to tell her. Dawn said, "It's OK Mum. I have read the book."

Dawn was married on 17th October 1949 to Kerry Byrne at St Joseph's Catholic Church. During this time, there was a huge Union strike for many people in Sydney. Preparing for her wedding, my father found it very hard to acquire alcohol. No beer! Not great for Irish descendants at all.

My father took the opportunity to take a job at Leo Buring Wines. Needless to say - you guessed it - the wedding guests were served champagne. No one asked any questions. They enjoyed the indulgence of the best champagnes.

The wedding was a joyous affair. The bridal party surnames were O'Sullivan, Maloney, Byrne and Kelly. Such an Irish affair.

Dawn, having had her children, went to work at A.W.A which was an electronics company. She worked in the office and assisted the punch card operators. The punch card, which had information and data on it, was loaded into the card reader. As time passed, the card system was done away with and the Computer Age proper was born. Dawn contributed to this age of technology.

My three brothers went to the Christian Brothers College. My sister and I attended the Good Samaritan Convent School, which, by the way, is still there. We would soon move down to Austinmer to live and I finished my schooling at St Mary's College in Wollongong. My daughter Donna also attended the same school and Freyja, my granddaughter, started there in 2021. Three generations attending the same school! Charley, my grandson, is attending Edmund Rice College in Wollongong. My son, Adam, went to Holy Spirit College. He now lives in Iceland with his wife Karen and my two granddaughters, Briet and Soley. They attend Flataskoli School.

Billy Maloney (Receiving communion at Mass before going into battle).

Rounding off our family tree: Billy and Betty - eight children, twenty-one grandchildren and twenty-three great grandchildren; Leo and Noelene - five children, eleven grandchildren and nine great grandchildren; Kevin and Carmel - six children, seven grandchildren and five great grandchildren; Dawn and Kerry - six children, fourteen grandchildren and nineteen great grandchildren; Margaret and Ray - two children and four grandchildren.

My life growing up was simple, yet joyous. The absolute security of my childhood was my environment. I had the most beautiful siblings and my family were, and still are, very important to me. It is everything. It is my history and without history, there is no future!

Without creativity, how can we exist?

And then it all started

I left school and went to work for Dr Bunn - who I am sure is looking down on us. To me, he was a saint. It was a great job and only five minutes from our home. It was on the corner of Lawrence Hargrave Drive and Cochrane Road, Thirroul. Thirroul means 'The Valley of the Palms.' It was paradise to me.

Dr Bunn's surgery was in his house. His wife was such a lovely person. She often made our morning tea.

After a short while working for Dr Bunn, he asked me if I would like to join the choir. Dr Bunn also happened to be the choirmaster at St Michael's Catholic Church at Thirroul. He had a baby grand piano in his house and sometimes during lunch, he would teach me to sing. With his encouragement, I joined the choir to learn more. The rhythm was always there. Not only did we learn to sing in English, but we also learnt to sing in Latin. I ended up singing the mass for my brother Kevin's wedding and also for the wedding of Ray's cousin, Gordon. I learnt so much from Dr Bunn.

I joined the Catholic Youth Organisation. (C.Y.O as it was called) where I met some very nice people. We had some fun times - picnics, house parties, car rallies and dances. It was all great for us young ones.

Around this time, my Aunt Neta and her children travelled down from Lithgow to Manly for a holiday. She would do this each year, and we would always visit them. She and my mother, who were sisters, were the best cooks in the world. Whilst visiting Aunt Neta, I fractured my ankle falling as I was coming down some stairs. The doctor told me that after my ankle had healed to do some exercises and suggested that there was no better way to exercise than to dance.

I was allowed to attend a ballroom dance class at Thirroul R.S.L and guess who my teacher was? Ray Reeve, the love of my life! I enjoyed the class so much. It was at that moment I knew what I wanted to do. So, I booked in for a private lesson each week for a half an hour's duration, after work. I would end up training with Ray for my medals.

The lesson cost me twelve shillings and sixpence. After the lesson, I would walk home to Austinmer. As I walked through the park next to our home, I would practice my walking and elevation exercises.

I was seventeen years of age when I was allowed to go with my brother Kevin to the weekly Saturday night dance at the Thirroul R.S.L. I loved it so much, because I got to dance with Ray in the progressive barn dance.

I needed some proper dance shoes, but at the time, ballroom dance shoes were not available in the shops, only tap and ballet shoes. I had a lovely pair of leather shoes with a nice heel in the colour of British racing green. I took them to a bootmaker to add some suede to the bottom. It prevented them from slipping and allowed me to dance.

After that, I had my shoes made by him. They were whatever colour I required. They were styled at the time with toe peepers and he was so excited that he used my style of shoe to make others, and he would reimburse me with the cost of mine. The heel was slightly thicker than today's dancing shoes - no stilettos. I had seen this style of shoe in an English Dance Journal offering information on dance. The boot maker was Coombs Shoe Repair in the Strand Arcade in Pitt Street, Sydney. The shop is still there, but with different owners, of course.

I started to dance competitively with a young man called Reg Martin, but it didn't last. Soon, I would have a new partner called André Young. André was a great dancer and a good friend. Ray trained us and we were very successful. We went from beginner to 1st place in an A Grade Final in twelve months, where we won the Amateur Modern. André was a wonderful dancer with a clear head, rhythmical and a good mover. We would practice every night.

Fortunately, but not in a bad way, Andre had wanderlust and wanted to travel and see the world. So, our partnership ended. We remained good friends for the rest of his life. A very sad passing.

After having made my first dress, a soft tangerine, I made a red one. After I finished one of my early competitions in the red dress, Ray said, "you want to burn that one," so I did!

Two weeks later, he asked where the red dress was? I told him I burnt it, as he suggested. He was so embarrassed. I wanted to do whatever I could to further my dancing and I thought that if the dress was that bad; I did as I was advised. Having total belief in my teacher.

From there, I started making all the dresses for the girls in the studio. They were so lucky. I got into a warehouse called SEWARDS and could buy material at cost price. The girls saved hundreds of pounds. I could then buy their sequins and diamantes as well.

One of the fashion houses in Wollongong at the time was Phil Jacobs Haute Couture. They heard about me and commissioned me to make an Evening Ball Gown (not Ballroom) which I did. It was such a nerve racking and wonderful experience for such a young person. The shop was of such high fashion. I ended up really loving it.

F.A.T.D was the Federal Association of Teachers of Dancing, of which later I studied hard and became an examiner. Eileen Kane was the secretary at the time. She was the best organiser ever! Everything was done with such class. She was 100 years old when she passed away. No one could ever fill a hall like she could.

The F.A.T.D Championships would run for three consecutive Saturdays from 6pm - 12pm. Sometimes it would start a bit earlier, but always on time. I might add that the best Professionals would partner their Medalists from their dance studios. Five Medalists would be on the floor at once. Identities like Ray and Judy Rivers, Ron and Jackie Nash, Jan Blanch and Peter Kelly. They were all from the Latin Branch. Then we had Ray Reeve, Kevin Calderon, Charles Froulop, Ivy Paton and Frank Northcote from the Modern Branch, just to name a few. They were all dance lovers.

To swap the styles around and for variety, Eileen would have the Modern Professional, Amateur New Vogue and the Junior Latin Open Championships in the first week, including supporting competitions, plus the Medalists.

For the second Saturday, there would be the Professional New Vogue, Amateur Latin, the Junior Modern and, once again, supporting competition grades, plus the Medalists. Week three would be the Professional Latin, Amateur Modern and the Junior New Vogue Open Championships, plus all the supporting events. Once again, everything ran on time.

Eileen had seen me doing my medals with Ray and suggested to him to dance with me. Maybe she could see something there. Just before Eileen passed away, I think Adam was about eight years of age. I had to go into the Federal Office in Pitt Street, Sydney. If ever he came with me, Eileen always called Adam her boyfriend. She loved him. They had a great rapport.

Eileen Kane retired in 1984 after 37 years at the helm of the F.A.T.D. At the invitation of the Board of Directors, to fill the role of Organising secretary (subsequently CEO) Robert J. Steele (Bob), relocated with his family to Sydney from Brisbane.

Bob's involvement with the F.A.T.D. commenced with his first teaching degree in 1963 and progressed with studies over the years until being appointed an Examiner in Ballroom, Latin and New Vogue. In 1972, he became the second youngest person ever to attain Fellowship degrees with F.A.T.D.

Bob brought with him a wealth of knowledge and experience. He began dancing as a young child, then continued through his years as an amateur competitor. He then became professional, along with his wife, Leigh. He also studied overseas and has judged many international competitions. Bob also represented Australia in other international ballroom dancing associations.

In Australia, Bob was heavily involved with staging many competitive dancing events, including State Championships and several South Pacific Championships, which at the time were the largest of all National Championships in the country. This stood him in good stead for the many promotions he handled whilst at the helm of the association.

Both prior to and during his F.A.T.D. term of office, Bob represented the Federal in administrative roles. First, with the Australian Dancing Board (previously ADBC) he was secretary for five years and served two terms as chairman. Later, with Dancesport Australia, he was a founding member in 1985 and served in the roles of Board of Director and Chairman of the Rules and Accreditation Committees.

Starting in 1989 and lasting for 27 years, Bob represented the F.A.T.D. and Dancesport generally in NSW in the role of referee to the BIG BROTHER MOVEMENT which provided financial assistance totaling $445,000, allowing NSW couples to travel to England to participate in the British Championships. His leadership role with the Federal Association lasted for 23 years until his retirement in 2007.

The Big Brother Movement was established in 1925 to provide a means for the settlement of large numbers of British lads applying to migrate to Australia at that time. The movement's founder was Sir Richard Linton and with the help of others, saw the need of an organisation to help youngsters of working age with financial assistance. This movement grew and eventually it would help

Australians who wanted to go to England with their expenses. It could have been in the arts, medical assistance, or other ventures. The Big Brother Movement eventually moved into the ballroom arena to help dancing couples. Hence, the term Big Brother (as a big brother would lend a helping hand). Much different to George Orwell, who wrote 1984, which was about how Big Brother is watching you.

The basic idea was to provide financial assistance to talented young Australians to enable them to undertake additional training and experience in Britain. Many young people have received help from this great organisation.

I have been informed that 41 couples from Australia have received the Big Brother Movement Award. Without that help, many couples would not have been able to travel to continue their development. Thirteen talented couples from our studio have received the award. I am personally very grateful for the help the Big Brother Movement provided to our studio.

It's up to us to decide who we are.

A new partner - Ray and I

So, we started dancing together and formed a successful partnership. Ray and I would practice every day from 10 am till 12 noon. I always made an assertion that a little, a lot, was better than a lot a little. We maintained muscles had no brains, so they had to be reminded every day what to do. Like a basketball player who needs to shoot hundreds of shots each day to get better and maintain accuracy. From here, I quickly got my confidence and started teaching.

My first pupil was Kerry Wilson. Kerry ended up becoming a great dancer - one of Australia's best. At eighteen, he won the Australian Amateur Championships. At twenty-two, he made the grand final of the World Amateur Modern at Sydney Town Hall, representing Australia with his cousin Maureen Wilson. All this and with no overseas training.

Our first professional competition was in 1962, at Sydney Town Hall. Ray and I ran third in the National Titles. We were so elated. I remember I wore a lovely mauve dress, covered in silver sequins that were hand sewn on by my wonderful mother. She was such a great person.

The next competition was the Medallist Travel Club Championships at The Southern Cross Hotel, Melbourne, for which we won this great big cup. It stood on the floor - so lovely. This cup was the one that we had a photograph taken with our son Adam when he was a toddler, sitting inside it. From here on, everything was happening.

Our first couple to win an Australasian championship was James Anderson and Dawn Salisbury. They won the Australasian Junior Championships in New Zealand. You might say, our first international winners.

Ray and Margaret Reeve.

Some of the best dancers that I taught started out as Juniors. They paid for a 15-minute lesson each fortnight. Generally, though, their lessons would go much longer. We would often let them come to classes for free. We wanted to encourage them with their dancing as we could see how talented they were. There was Kerry Wilson, Doug Newton, Donald Wood and James (Jimmy) Anderson. Even though he was young, Jimmy was Donald Wood's uncle. They were all accomplished dancers and were partnered with lovely girls.

Kerry danced with Dianne Dryden. Doug danced with Maureen McCauley. Don with Merrilyn Royall, who he later married and Jimmy Anderson with Dawn Salisbury. Another couple, Rosalyn Toulmin and John Oliver, came into the mix later.

To start with, lessons for our couples comprised a half an hour single individually, and a one-hour lesson per couple over Modern and Latin. That was quite different to how lessons are run today. The teacher and student lessons quickly elevated their understanding and feel for the dances. The standard was much better overall. We taught lots of single lessons as well, for the medalists who did not have partners.

I always thought that there were three ways that one learns - by feel, by looking and by talking. How? One without the other wasn't any good. Hence, the half hour single lesson really helped. This was the only way we knew, and it seemed to work for us. We tried so hard to produce champions.

Our Saturday morning class was fantastic. Nearly all of our budding champions came out of that class and paved the way for many talented dancers.

Having done some teaching at our first studio in Raymond Road, we were offered a more suitable room on the next corner, at Number 2, McCauley Street. The McCauley Street studio was completed and we were very trusting in our decision to move across. The parents of one of our pupils owned the premises. The deal was that we give the builder, who was renowned locally, 3,000 pounds as rent paid in advance. Ray went over to the bank and drew out the money. It was Saturday morning, as the banks were open then. I ran our Saturday morning class and overnight; the builder went bankrupt. A lesson learnt about trust. We lost the money!

Ray and Margaret Reeve.

That did not stop us, as we managed to stay on. We were successful and carried on teaching and competing in this new studio. Many champions were created at McCauley Street. I was once told that as you get older; you become wiser - I don't know about that! Thinking differently, not just about what you can do, but how you do it, will help you find new ways to apply your strengths.

You can't take anyone there (to success) if you haven't been there yourself and that was certainly true with our teacher. Ray and I trained under Henry Jacques. He was a great teacher, the best in the world. He taught us minimum effort for maximum effect. One did not dance with physical effort - it was controlled.

Henry, or as we would address him, Mr. Jacques, came out to Australia from England. He, along with two other English teachers, Josephine Bradley and Phyllis Haylor, are credited as pioneers and who were instrumental in the invention of Modern Ballroom Dancing. We understood his teaching methods explicitly. He would teach his theories by explaining the amount of energy used by a professional painter or golfer.

One night we were attending a dinner held for dance teachers, along with Mr. and Mrs. Jacques. Henry gave a speech during which he said, "Ray and I would be the next top teachers." We were so surprised that he said that.

Henry started off the teaching methods - advancing technique. Len Scrivener filled in the missing links to the next level. They were both historically wonderful. We had good production methods of teaching, which hopefully, we have passed on.

A funny story that should be told. We were at a competition one day. It was a small one and Henry Jacques was the sole adjudicator. As the afternoon progressed and they went through the rounds, Henry stopped the competition and announced in his beautiful English accent, "Ladies and gentlemen, there seems to be some mistake. Couple number 45 keeps appearing in the next round of competition and as sole adjudicator, I have not chosen them from the first round." It appears their teacher was the scrutineer and kept putting his couple into the next round. Highly unprofessional, but very characteristic of the scrutineer.

We studied hard under Ivy Paton for theory and Charles Froulop for practical. We sat for our exams. The examinations started at Associate (Level 1). Then one would have to wait two years, as you continued studying for your Membership. Then you had to wait another two years and if you wanted to, you would continue studying for your Fellowship. The Fellowship was the highest examination one could take if you were successful in doing so.

If you counted up the years without a break, it would be seven. I think that is about the same as a lawyer. Then, to become an examiner of the Federal Association, one had to be appointed by the governing body. I received my appointment as an examiner at twenty-eight. Apparently, I am the youngest Fellow and Examiner of the F.A.T.D.

If dancing is your passion, consider a new life partner.

Ray's family

In 1924, Ray's mother Elsie Madigan married William Reeve. Elsie was raised by her aunt and uncle Fairhall, who ran the Bulli Lookout Kiosk that provided light refreshments. William Fairhall was the lessee and Elsie would help out at the Kiosk on the weekends.

In 1927, The Duke and Duchess of York embarked on a tour of Australia. They arrived March 26 aboard *HMS RENOWN*, a battleship that was fitted out to accommodate The Duke and Duchess and their entourage. It would be a hectic schedule of political engagements and sightseeing.

The Royal Couple were very busy on their planned trip and had visited the Jenolan Caves. They were delighted at the beauty and surroundings of the Blue Mountains. They were also scheduled to visit Bulli Pass and the South Coast and Elsie was excited at the prospect of the Royal couple coming to the kiosk. Unfortunately, The Duke and Duchess were not able to make time to visit. However, the opportunity was taken to organise tours for the officers and men of the *HMS RENOWN*. The officers visited the tea-room, as it was sometimes called, and remarked on the beautiful scenery of the area. They had never seen anything like it before. It was a wonderful experience for them.

Ray's mother and father were also interested in dancing. During the depression, as good people who helped out, they ran a Saturday night dance at a venue called The Kookaburra Hall, in Thirroul. Admission for the dance was sixpence, which included a cup of tea and biscuits.

Ray's father, Bill, was the MC for the dance. Ray's mother would play the piano and she would put Ray in a bassinet underneath while she played. I suppose his rhythm came from having that piano playing hammered into him. They were really thoughtful about the way they helped people during the depression. It was 1931 and such a hard time for everyone.

The Kookaburra Hall had its own band called the Kookaburra Orchestra. Ray's mother was also a part of it. Ray's mother, Elsie, had been playing piano for quite some time. She used to play piano for Old-Time Dances that were held on a Saturday night at the Thirroul Railway Hall, as part of their social club, back in the late 20s. I was also told that Elsie, occasionally, would play piano for the silent movies when they were being shown in town.

Dances were a regular thing back in those days. It was so much a part of everyday life. They were used as get-togethers, monthly events and even charity fundraisers. Sporting clubs would hold a fundraiser dance. Clubs and other organisations would do the same for various reasons. It gave young people a chance to go out, get dressed up, meet and have a good time. They generally cost very little to attend, and they supplied many of them with a light supper or refreshments during the night. They were frequented a lot!

Originally, the Kookaburra Hall was The Arcadia Theatre, but it only remained a cinema for three years. After that it was sold and turned into a dance hall until 1943. Bill Reeve would MC many such dances for years to come, which earned him the nickname Bill JAZZER Reeve.

Elsie and Bill Reeve were very community-oriented people. When Ray was a young boy, his parents ran a mixed business that sold deli items, grocery lines, fruit and vegetables. It was situated on Lawrence Hargrave Drive, Thirroul, opposite Ryan's famous hotel. They served the community for several years.

What they probably remembered mostly about Ray's father was the fact that he was captain of the Thirroul Fire Brigade. Bill Reeve joined the fire brigade as a volunteer in 1925 and eventually he became a paid firefighter. He was Captain for 25 years and lived next door to the station, which I might add is still there and beautifully looked after.

People often speak about their awards, but none more famous than Ray's father. In 1962, he was invited to Government House and was presented an O.B.E (ORDER OF THE BRITISH EMPIRE) by the Governor on behalf of Queen Elizabeth II. A very prestigious award and very well received. We were and still are very proud of him.

When WWII hit England with The Blitz in London, he offered to go to help fight the fires. The officials, however, would not send him because they said his expertise was required here in Australia.

I must add a brief comment here. When we first got married, we lived with Ray's parents for six months before moving into our home. I can remember that darn fire alarm going off at night time. I would almost exorcise right off the bed about six feet.

Elsie's brother, Wally Madigan, first taught Ray how to dance. Ray's Uncle Wally was also a military man. He served in WWI as part of the Anzac Cyclist Battalion and he was also a horse driver. They widely used horses during the war and were instrumental in the movement of soldiers and supplies throughout. He was also of service during WWII in Australia for several months.

Wally Madigan began teaching in Sydney from 1940. He came down to Wollongong and began teaching in 1949 and opened his own school at Thirroul. He was well known throughout Australia as a dance teacher.

In Thirroul, Wally first taught at the hall in Railway Parade called the Thirroul Railway Institute Hall, which is now a heritage site. He then moved to the Thirroul R.S.L. Club to teach and continue the dancing.

His dance school, along with his students, became very successful in a short period of time. Wally held many local dancing festivals - competitions. He would run them with other local teams and with couples competing against each other. Often the day would start out with Medal examinations with competitions during the night. The day finished with a professional demonstration from well-known dancers in the industry.

Wally's student Medalists were either S.A.T.D, A.T.D or F.A.T.D. These organisations are still running Medal tests and competitions to high standards. Some of the examiners at the time were Don Lucas, Mrs Misdale, Stephen Hughes, Bob Potter, Penelope Cay and Ron Doyle.

Wally would sometimes bring Sydney teams to compete against his local teams at his Dancing Festivals, where the competitions were judged by leading Sydney dance teachers such as Eileen Kane, Bob Potter and Ivy Paton. Wally's students also competed in larger ballroom competitions, including state and interstate championships, where Wally was also a judge.

In 1949, the S.A.T.D. association, together with The Modern Ballroom Teachers Association Canberra, staged The Gala Championship Dance. This included medal tests at 2.30pm and commencing at 8pm was The Gala Championship Event. It was held on November 4th, in conjunction with the Country Championships.

Competitors from Wollongong, Thirroul, Liverpool, Young, Austinmer and Canberra took part in these Championships. It was called the Canberra and S.A.T.D Championships and the Country Championships. They also ran a teams' match at this event - Canberra versus Parramatta - in formation dancing. As a side note, my partner Andre Young and I won the Country Championships at the Paddington Town Hall, Sydney, at a later date.

The Canberra Championships were organised by Mr. James O'Halloran and Moyra O'Neill. Judges from Sydney, Parramatta, Wollongong, Thirroul and Albury officiated. A very successful event and is part of the commencement of our early history of Ballroom Dancing.

In 1954, Canberra hosted their inclusion into the Australasian Championships. Representatives were chosen to dance in the Australasian Championships by each state and New Zealand. In that year, they held it in New Zealand. One hundred couples competed in the Championships that the S.A.T.D. ran.

With Ray's Uncle Wally Madigan originating ballroom dancing in Thirroul, Ray had other relatives who were a part of the Ballroom Dancing scene. Gordon Reeve, who was Ray's cousin, also danced at the Thirroul Hall and would help out on the line. The line was a beginner class where the students would sit down, awaiting their turn to dance. Gordon would take each student and teach them the steps in front of the others, awaiting their turn. Ray was in charge of the music and would run in between, put the record on and then come back to teach another student.

Gordon Reeve worked with us at our first two studios. He was an amateur competitor and would sometimes help with the lessons. He eventually turned professional with local girl Margaret Cochrane. Gordon and Margaret eventually married and left the area for Nowra. They opened a successful dance studio that operated for many years. They ran social dancing and also had competition dancers.

Back in the day, Wally's sister Irene and her husband, Victor Samuels, ran dances at The Albert Hall in Canberra. The Albert Hall is a heritage listed building that was opened in 1928. The Albert Hall ran many events, including exhibitions, displays, conferences, presentations, concertos and the like. The one thing that The Albert was well known for were the dances and the balls that they held. The building is well cared for and continues to serve the community.

You can't do everything, you can't do nothing,
but you can do something!

One learns something every day.

1961

We had a very successful year with our lovely couples. To top it off, Ray and I were married at St Michael's Catholic Church, Thirroul, on December 2nd. Joy Smith was my bridesmaid, another great dancer, who danced with her brother, Neville. They were the most adult couple in our studio. My three little nieces were the flower girls. I think they were all absolutely beautiful. One blonde, one brunette and one auburn. Kevin, my brother, was the best man and Father Brambly was the officiating priest.

We held our wedding reception at the Thirroul R.S.L. Hall. A lot of our dancing friends attended as well. The entertainment was great. A demonstration by our dear friends Jimmy and Betty Maschmedt of exhibition dancing entertained everyone. They were so classy and good. Actually, they were the last to leave our wedding reception along with my brothers around 3 am - the following morning.

Ray loved his fishing. One day, we decided to go down to Lake Illawarra to fish. We hired a little boat and away we went. It was a beautiful day. However, the weather changed with squally winds and black clouds started to hover. We tried to start the boat - it didn't start. So, we rowed the boat toward the shore, but the storm kept taking us away from our destination. We finally made it to shore, about 2 miles away from our starting position. We dragged the boat to shore and started to walk back. Luckily for us, some other people in another boat came out looking for us and they managed to collect our boat and bring it in. We were okay and were able to walk back to the boathouse. That day, I learnt words I had never heard before in all my life.

If we were free, Ray and I never hesitated to just pack up the car late on a Saturday afternoon and take off anywhere into the country.

We would often spend the night beside a small rivulet and cook our meals on a little gas stove that we had. We would sleep in the back of our station wagon on the blow-up beds. It was very adventurous. In the morning, we would cook bacon and eggs for breakfast.

In our haste, however, on one of our trips, we forgot the food. We had one packet of rice-a-riso in the car - so we ate that. Right next to where we had parked were many blackberry bushes, so that's what we had for breakfast. After breakfast, we drove into a little town in the Araluen Valley and had a meal at the old hotel. We really enjoyed our little adventures. We then built our home and moved in February 1962.

One Easter after we were married, Ray went away fishing. I did not go with him as my mother was very sick in Coledale Hospital. I stayed at home so I could visit her, which I did every day. Our house was the first one built in the estate. My dad stayed with me for company. There was a bush all around us.

Ray had left me his gun, a 22 single shot for security - pretty basic. (He also lent this lovely keepsake to a friend and never got it back). However, during the night, I heard a rustle in the bushes next to our house and so I opened fire into the bushes, not knowing who or what it was. On returning, Ray asked me if I went to see if I had shot anything or anyone. Thank God I hadn't!

We used to love going down the coast. On one trip we happened upon an old farm. It was just beautiful. There was no one there. Ray tried to teach me how to fire a 303 rifle. The force of the rifle nearly threw me into the bush. Big mistake. The rifle was too strong for me. It nearly blew my shoulder off.

So, we went wandering across the open field and we saw this huge bull in the distance. We didn't think he could see us, but he did. So, we thought it was time to move. We ran and he chased us. He was much faster than us. He was winning. Then we saw this hedge in front of us. Our hearts were in our mouths. He was so big. The hedge got closer, and so did the bull. We had no escape. We ran straight through the hedge, leaving an imprint through it! As we did, the bull followed us but came to a standstill on the other side of the hedge. A close call indeed!

On another trip down to the Araluen Valley and being a city girl, I was in a rapture for this beautiful country of ours. We went shooting rabbits and if we were lucky enough, we would cook them with some potatoes in a camp oven for dinner.

Strolling through the bush, I spotted a rabbit up on the hill. So, with the little single shot, I fired at the rabbit and he fell down. It was a hundred yards away. So, I asked Ray if he would get it for me. His reply was, "Don't be silly, he probably fell into his burrow." "Well, aren't you going to have a look?" I said.

So, Ray went all the way up the hill and retrieved the rabbit, only to find that I had shot it straight between the eyes, a hundred yards away with a single shot.

Those little trips were our escape from the business on a Saturday afternoon and Sunday if we weren't working.

Goodness is so attractive and so rare.

True goodness is irresistible to me.

1965: The World's and the British

When I began to dance, Latin American dancing wasn't part of the studio format. In fact, not many studios offered it. It wasn't until around the early 1960s that it was properly introduced into the ballroom curriculum. It was about this time that we introduced it into our studio. When I danced with Andre, we only did Modern, as that was all that was taught at the studio, along with old time that is now called New Vogue. Even with just those two styles, the competitions were huge and many wanted to learn to dance.

In December 1962, The World Professional Ballroom Championships were held for the very first time at the Festival Hall in Melbourne, Australia. There were competitors from England, Germany, Japan, New Zealand and, of course, Australia. All the Australian competitors had to dance in the early rounds. It was a huge and rigorous event where one had to dance both styles. Unfortunately, I wasn't feeling very well. Even though we had made it through to the rounds of the Modern section, Ray thought it was best not to go on any further. So, with much disappointment, we pulled out of the competition. Yet, it was this particular competition that gave us a greater drive to compete against the best dancers in the world. We really wanted to learn and take our dancing further.

The following year, 1963, as part of their promotion, the A.N.D.A selected Ray and me to be part of their Professional Team to tour England - just like the last one when the late Mickey Powell was the captain. This time, Joe Love was the captain. This was the championship where we were placed third, and as part of this promotion were invited to join the team. However, as things happen, they brought Arthur and Linda Cornwell out of retirement and replaced us with them. They were fine dancers, but we felt very disappointed. I guess that's how the cookie crumbles. Sometimes one just has to get on with it. We then went it alone, as one might say.

Sometime later, we were chosen by the then Board of Control to represent Australia at the World Ballroom Dancing Championships to be held in England in 1965. They held this event in London at Wembley Pool - a magnificent place. We were to represent both the Modern and the Latin. Ray and I felt quite excited about this. After all, it was England, the Mecca of ballroom dancing. It was such a great honour to represent the country. We were ready to burst - our first international competition of such high acclaim!

The trip was highly expensive. With no contributions towards our costs, we had to do it on our own. One of our professional friends raised some money for us - money lost in transit. The only thing received from our peers was a telegram message that said *KEEP THE FLAG FLYING*. It almost sounded like someone was a comedian. Not to be deterred, we focused on the positive. Our coaches, friends and pupils all wished us well. That meant more to us.

Fortunately, a little help from two local businesses. The first was a referral from our local bank, The Commonwealth, with whom we had a great relationship, owned a flat in Maida Vale, just down from Marble Arch, Oxford Street end. The caretaker of the apartment was Mrs Rapson. We were able to rent the flat, which was really convenient. The lounge room of the flat was so big that sometimes, after our lessons during the day, we would practice in there at night, running through what we learned that day. The second business to help us was the local newspaper from Wollongong, The Mercury, which gave us a press card, enabling us to gain admittance anywhere whilst representing The Mercury.

So, we planned our trip to England. We gave ourselves three months to not only compete in The World Championships but also The British Open. We scheduled extra lessons, a little sightseeing and vacation time as well.

We flew to London from Australia, stopping in Rome - something I had always dreamt of, but never thought it would happen! Staying at Hotel Quirinale, we spent a few days on sightseeing, visiting Saint Peter's Basilica, the catacombs and wanting to visit the Sistine Chapel. Unfortunately, being Easter, it was closed. Nevertheless, we got to see it in later years. This was an exciting prelude to our stay in London. The churches, statues and monuments were astounding, all balanced in size.

Every sports person has that longing to be good enough to represent one's country internationally in a World Championship. This was our dream come true - to compete with world class dancers! It was so exciting. Some countries had adjudicators selected to represent them. Unfortunately, we did not. But that did not matter.

In the vast arena of the Wembley Pool, crowds estimated over the two nights of the competition were close to 18,000! The 1965 event may well go down in history as one of the most daringly conceived, most excellently run, World Championships of all time. It was a lively and colourful spectacle of the finest dancers competing for the great honour of winning the supreme title of champion of the world for their country.

The music over the two evenings was provided by those superb bands, Joe Loss and Ken Mackintosh. Rarely dancers in The World Championships would have competed to such wonderful music. Incidentally, we used to practice with those bands at the famous Hammersmith Palais. They would run practice sessions every night. On a Tuesday night, a top line couple could demonstrate in competition attire. Those of us who were practicing would be dressed elegantly, ladies in lovely dresses that flowed as they danced and men fittingly dressed in their suits.

It was unique that both the Amateur and Professional World Championships in both Modern and Latin were run at the same time at Wembley. Such great dancing and with such enthusiasm.

Something that we were very proud of was leading the couples out onto the floor at the 1965 World Championships. We were number 3 and Australia was the first country announced onto the floor. As usual, a helper held our flag, standing in front of us. The other competing couples formed a large v shape during the announcement. We danced the Viennese waltz onto the floor, opening the World Championships. As a side note: we studied with Von Eichler for our Viennese waltz after the Championships. He had expert knowledge, simplicity and know-how. He also gave us his notes that I often refer to in my teaching.

There was a revolution in the choreography never seen before - throwaway oversway, aeros line, bombshell, change of mind lunge, overspin, double Spanish drag (tango) and jump contra check. Things were executed differently. Amalgamations were lovely. Theories in the quickstep were quite exciting. Being new to the world, the people in Australia had seen none of this before.

We made some lovely friends - Anthony and Fay Hurley, George and Patricia Coad, John and Betty Westley, Maurice and Dolly Strowbridge, Rudi and Mechthild Trautz and Makato and Toshi Seki. Anthony Hurley, along with Sonny Binick, helped Ray with his tail fittings (a newly constructed set with the newer, shorter length).

We had such a good connection with everyone, taking in so much and gaining knowledge, which continued on from Henry's teachings. It was all going with us, loving it and to have Anthony and Fay, now living in Australia. Such a lovely couple. Ray Rivers prepared us for our Latin in the World championships, coming 7th in both styles - confirmation of where we ran kept in our archives.

We received just as much prize money as the winners of the Latin - Walter and Marianne Kaiser from Switzerland. They were not the favourites to win, but they were the best.

At the World Championships Seki beat us. In the British, we finished ten places ahead of him. The organisers got my name mixed up. I don't know how, but they listed me as Margaret Reynolds. One of my students from Perth, who would eventually come over to our studio to further his learnings, used to say to me, "Hello Miss Reynolds." That was Brett Dorney, a very fine dancer.

And so, it was. After the World Championships, we continued learning from our select teachers, Len Scrivener, Sonny Binick, Bill Irvine, Nina Hunt, Doris Lavelle, Peter Eggleton and Sydney Francis. Wow! What a broad line of learning!

One night, we were invited to demonstrate at Penge in Kent in the Royston Ballroom owned by Frank and Peggy Spencer, the very famous formation team teachers. It was their Seniors` night, so we thought this wouldn't be so nerve racking, only to learn that Billy and Bobbie Irvine had demonstrated there the week before. Shock horror! The hall was packed, but they really loved our show.

To get to Penge meant catching the train. As anyone who has travelled with a ballroom dress and net petticoats, at that time of night, would understand it was a pain in the butt.

However, they invited us to go with their team to Blackpool by bus for the British Championships. It was similar to when our own studio travelled to the Australian Championships. Their students were pleasant, wanting to know everything about Australia. Peggy booked our accommodation, etc. Making it so much easier for us. (Peggy Spencer also coached Rudolf Nureyev in the Tango for the 1977 movie *Valentino*).

We would go to the practice sessions at the Winter Gardens` magnificent ballroom. The British Championships, considered the

Wimbledon of ballroom dancing, ran for one week. Each day we would practice and if lucky enough to get through to the rounds, dance in the competition at night. We were.

At Winter Gardens, Blackpool, on walking into the Ballroom, the atmosphere was electric. It was just so exciting. The floor was much bigger and beautiful to dance on. There were no seats available. They had sold all the tickets. We were so lucky that Mrs. Illett, who was the organiser at the time, found two seats in the front row for us. Two people had cancelled because of ill health. We ended up sharing them with our friends. Years later, we would have our own box at Winter Gardens. It was so good.

The night we danced was at the end of the week. Scrivener gave us a practice group in the Quickstep. When asked what we should start with in the Quickstep for the competition, he said, "That one." It had everything in it for ease of movement. We moved like the wind around that floor. To this day, we still use that group, making many variations to its foundation. Scrivener said that Quickstep comprises walks and chasses. That is the foundation of your Quickstep.

So, we made the twenty-four, just missing out on the twelve and being placed 15th. We improved a lot during our time in England and we're so proud of our achievements. Some couples just go on the trip when travelling overseas for dancing, but we worked our butts off. There was so much to learn, not only the dancing but also the broader aspect and approach.

The British Championships had begun their running in 1920, the programme featuring competition only in Old Time Sequence Dancing. In 1926, the Modern Ballroom segment was introduced. With the onset of World War II, the championships were postponed. As part of the 1975 Championships at the Welcoming Party for the English and overseas visitors, one of our representatives, Bob Steele, made the Welcoming Speech for Australia. This was considered a great honour.

When we were to come back from Blackpool, Sonny Binick and his father-in-law offered us a lift back to London. They drove a vintage Jaguar and so we accepted, of course.

On one occasion, Sonny Binick was competing in Germany. He was very successful and won the event. It was a tremendous competition. With tongue in cheek, I'll tell a brief story about Sonny.

In Germany at the time, the English dancers usually won. They got the marks, but the German dancers received the prizes. Results were announced first and then the prizes were awarded separately. The presenter had a beautiful television set which he was about to present to the German couple in 2nd place. Sonny stepped out and rather smartly, received the trophy saying, "Thank you very much." The presenter was shocked. Sonny knew what was going on. Later the presenter said to Sonny, "Mr. Binick, you will never be invited back to Germany again." Sonny's reply was, "That's okay. I wasn't invited the first time." I think he also told the presenter if he said anything else, he would throw him down the stairs.

Sonny fought during WWII for England. He was a paratrooper and fought at the battle of Arnhem, 97 kilometres east of Rotterdam, Netherlands, where casualties were heavy.

Whilst in London competing for The World's, we were invited to Alex Moore's place for supper where we met Makato and Toshi Seki for the first time. It was the start of a long and warm friendship. With a lovely new friendship started, they invited the four of us to Munich, Germany and we travelled there together. The trouble was Makato and Toshi couldn't speak English and we couldn't speak Japanese. However, we found a way to communicate.

We caught the train from Paddington station and then the organisers put us on a boat. We caught another train - during which we tried to make them feel comfortable. Ray was hilarious. He told Makato that he was Mickey Mouse and Ray was Donald Duck. They, as Japanese, laughed a lot!

Have you ever done anything that may come back to haunt you? Well, we did. We attended a reception the night before the competition, at which all the men were in black tie and suits and the ladies wore beautiful gowns. We were having a drink with Peter Eggleton, who arranged our trip, when Makato came down the stairs to join us. Much to everyone's surprise, he said in a loud voice, his hands pointing to his chest, "ME MICKEY MOUSE." The crowd clapped because he looked just like him.

Germany was still mourning, losing the war. It was a country now divided and cities needed rebuilding. On leaving Munich, it was necessary to get the train back to the boat. We did not know what platform to go to and no one would help us. The trains usually dropped off a carriage from the back end, depending where it was travelling to. We took a punt, coming up with the right decision. We had to look after our Japanese friends - a friendship we valued so much. Remember, this was 1965 and relationships between our two countries had changed.

In the 1988 Bicentenary Celebration of Australia, Ray Rivers organised and ran a great international competition. During the championship, two teams competed. The captains were Ray Reeve, Australia and Makato Seki from Japan. It was so lovely to see two old friends reunite. We have been friends for over 50 years.

They must have really liked our dancing in Munich because we received another invitation. This time it was to Leverkusen - but not to play soccer! We went with Dennis Udell and Joyce Brampton. This time they flew us from London to The Bayer Pharmaceutical Lodge in Leverkusen, near Dusseldorf. It was a magnificent venue. Our suite was so luxurious. We had two of everything. I have seen nothing like it in my life.

On their grounds, there was a garden from each country characterised in its own habitat. So beautiful! One could only imagine how large the grounds were to accommodate such luxury.

The competition was so amazing. During the Viennese Waltz, Dennis and Joyce sat down. Dennis said that they would not win that dance, so they sat down for a rest. Freddie (Fred) Dieselhorst, who was the German organiser, turned out to be the judge for the World Championships in Melbourne in 1967, representing Germany.

More information pertaining to the Viennese Waltz. The British do not have it. For them there are only four dances - Waltz, Foxtrot, Tango and Quickstep - in that order. For the World Championships, the organisers included the Viennese Waltz. The English considered the Viennese Waltz to be a folk dance and did not include it in their preparation for the prestigious British Championships. Hence, the 1965 British Championships were won by Peter and Brenda.

Makato and Toshi Seki wanted to have lessons with us while we were there, but we did not feel good about this, as like us, they too were learning from Sonny Binick. However, we checked it out and it was okay. I don't think Sonny minded. He was such an outstanding teacher and everyone loved him.

The Seki's used to watch us practice and loved my head application. It was not so much my head, but my sides that gave my styling a strong but balanced look. Every year when they competed in the All-Japan Championships, they would run 2nd to Shinoda. It was always the Foxtrot that cost them the competition. So, we danced with each of them to give them a feel for the dance and they responded. Well, they practiced and practiced what we showed and taught them and it really helped.

Back in Australia, before leaving on our way to an F.A.T.D executive meeting, the postman delivered a letter to us. It was from the Seki's. They had won the All-Japan Championships, beating Shinoda and they won the Foxtrot. They thanked us so much. The letter was so beautiful.

Ray and Margaret Reeve.

While studying in England, after the World Championships, we ran into a colleague from dancing. His name was Bruce Blanch and he invited Ray and me to go with him on a trip through Europe. We were so delighted to go - one of the most marvelous times we ever had! We flew to Bordeaux, then to Biarritz, San Sebastian and dined at one of the most famous restaurants in the world. People queued outside for ages to get a seat. The venue was like a long corridor - a skinny one. You could still taste the salt water in the seafood, it was so fresh.

From San Sebastian we went to Barcelona and onto San Feliu, intending to see a bullfight since there was none at that time in Barcelona. We stayed at a beautiful little villa for 50 cents a night, eventually getting to see the bullfight. Ray didn't go. It was fantastic, though we left before they killed the bull. El Cordobes was the matador. He was very famous.

The next leg of the trip took us to the Costa Brava, along the coastline of Spain, then to Naples, Baden- Baden and onto Montreux, Switzerland. We stayed at a lovely villa at Lac Lémon, which is known as Lake Geneva, right on the lake - a sight that everyone goes to see.

There was an English couple who came to the same hotel as us to see the lake. They had been coming for four years and this was their fifth year. They hadn't seen it before because of the fog. We told them, "You won't miss out this time. We saw it yesterday." And you guessed it! The nicest morning after breakfast, we all went outside to see the lake and the fog was back again.

The dancing fraternity had seen none of our new choreography. This was a great revolution. We never forgot our ease of movement which we incorporated in our recent work - steps that we brought back with us from England.

We arrived home in Australia on Thursday and we danced on the Saturday at the F.A.T.D. championships. Unusual, but we were itching to dance. It was at Marrickville Town Hall and it was packed to the rafters. People who came to see us were standing on extra seats made available - up against the wall.

We live our lives in patterns and rhythms, not seconds and minutes. Time is relaxed and you dictate your schedule. This is how my life has always been. Everything is self-timing. My life conceded the timing, and one might say, in a rhythmical manner. With design, excellence and quality built in, one is bound to find inspiration. Our inspiration? To dance in the British and represent in the World Championship.

When we learn how to use our bodies in our dancing, we can hack our true potential. I have always believed that you must have a dream and that you have to work hard to make it happen. Hence the inspiration of our dream. Stir your imagination!

One does not institute creativity, it happens!

New Zealand

After coming home from England, we went to New Zealand to compete in the South Pacific Championships. We were first in the Modern section and second in the Latin. The following year, they invited us back to demonstrate, teach and adjudicate.

On our first trip to New Zealand, to judge their National Titles and demonstrate, something happened as we were coming through the airport. We were aware of a man observing us. He had a hat on that was pulled down over his face and he was wearing an overcoat with the collar pulled up around his neck. We thought it was very strange. Like a big cloak and dagger incident. He was checking to see who spoke to us before the championships. Very strange. We knew who it was, but it didn't make any difference to us.

The tour, as we called it, was a very hardworking one. We toured both islands. We met some very lovely people. Mr. Len Marsden, who was the president of the New Zealand Federation, really loved us. He quoted in our dance review that New Zealand dancing had improved since our first visit. The revolution of the 1965 choreography was so exhilarating to them.

At the New Zealand Championships, something amazing happened. Ray and I saw this lovely couple from Dunedin. Their names were Ken and Joan Miller. They weren't the current champions in their grade, but to us on the day they were. We marked them to win, but they ran third. Hence my motto: If you are good enough, you will win!

Ken and Joan came to Australia to further their studies with us. They came for three months and stayed for three years. When they returned to New Zealand, they opened up a very successful dance academy. I have not in my lifetime seen such a hardworking lady as Joan - with a great personality.

Ken and Joan Miller.

We have always been a great influence on New Zealand dancing. They were so willing to learn. Their championship couples were lovely dancers and their love of dance was so giving. Peter and Wendy Smith were the New Zealand Amateur Modern and Latin Champions. They were lovely dancers. Peter and Wendy used to come over to Australia each year to represent New Zealand at the Australasian and do some work with us.

Peter and Wendy went to England to further their studies of dancing. I think, until Peta Roby came along, that Wendy did the best pot stirrer - a step in the Rumba. As things happen, Peter and Wendy separated. Peter then remarried Rosalyn Toulmin and to this day, they live in the beautiful Illawarra, having remained close friends. Peter and Rosalyn won the South Pacific Professional Modern Championships in New Zealand. They went to England to further their studies. Peter Smith became the top journalist for the Dancing Times.

We had a stream of great foundation New Zealanders - Candy Lane, Peter and Wendy Smith, Maurice and Judy Taylor, Jo Winiki, Ivy Biberstein, Gary and Margaret Wilson, Barry Gasson, Maurice and Barbara Edwards, Michael Nicholas, George Nicholls, Grant and Sheryl Macown, Gaile and Robin French, Gerald McAuley, Da Katipa, Patrick Corbett, Laurel and David Mayne. They engaged us with much enthusiasm.

We loved touring New Zealand and teaching there and have always been very well received. New Zealand is the most beautiful country.

I always said that one could measure one's ability in 3 stages in the winning arena - State, National and International. One's ability could be one of those things, or all of them.

Now a rather strange thing happened when we danced in the South Pacific, in Christchurch, New Zealand, 1965. The three top Australian couples in form were there to compete. Those being ourselves, Kevin Calderon and June Bratt and Cedric and Val Meers. The format was quite strange. The organisers on behalf of Federal (F.A.T.D.) thought they would run two Professional Modern Championship events as opposed to running just one, as was the norm. To this day, I don't know what their reasoning was for this. It just ended up being a DISASTER! I hope you can understand the following.

Peter and Wendy Smith.

Ray and I won the first one. However, the scrutineers stuffed up big time. By winning the first Championship there was no need for us to dance the second one. The winner of the first event would not have been permitted to dance in the second event. It left everyone else to compete again for the placings. We didn't know that, so we danced in the second event too. Now our name was not on the list for the second one and Kevin Calderon was at the top of the list to dance the second one and because of that, they thought he was the winner. So, they called him out as the winner of the first competition, so he did not have to dance the second.

That was a big Mistake! The media wrote for the newspapers that Kevin and June were the official winners - that was wrong. This left Cedric and Val well up in the air.

This mistake mixed up the prize money. We won both, but should not have danced in the second. Confused? Well, we were too! So, the three couples combined all the prize money from the first three places in both competitions and split it three ways. Reeve, Calderon and Meers. This was Ray's idea. I think we missed out a bit. This mistake was corrected and announced to the audience. We felt for the organisers.

Doug Newton and Maureen McCauley were the Junior Champions. As teachers and Australians, we tried to give our pupils confidence and we cheered for them and they also cheered for us.

Doug, a developing young man, was so excited to see Ray and I dancing. He cheered for us with much excitement. The promoter told him to stop. His response was, "They are my teachers and they have returned from England, representing Australia in the World's and the British Championships and I won't stop."

During one of our New Zealand lectures, Ray made a comment about a young man's shape and hold. Ray said he and his partner were the best-looking couple - until they started to dance. Someone then nicknamed *him 'Wristy'* because his left arm and wrist were so bad. However, everything went off fine. We loved the New Zealand dancers. They were eager and anxious to learn.

Twenty years later and still touring New Zealand, a young dancer asked me to do my isometric exercises for dancing. He was there for our very first lecture many years before. They thought I looked like a transformer. We were amazed we packed the venue to the rafters.

I still teach these exercises today. Pertaining to Latin, they help the body movement of flexibility and rhythm. Sydney Francis helped me with them and my Jive exercises. A lot of our exercises are the same as those used for ballet.

One year, we took 102 people from our studio to New Zealand for the South Pacific Championships. At the time, air fares for children under 12 years old only cost $50! It is not like that now. By the way, under 12 years didn't have to have a passport. We had so many under 12-year-old competitors with their parents.

After competing, we toured by bus for two weeks. One morning at The Hermitage Hotel at Mt Cook, all the pupils had a snow fight. The thing was, I was the target. From the snowfields, we climbed up and down via the chairlift.

We also caught a plane to take us through the mountains, landing on those beautiful snowfields. From there we went onto Queenstown. It was such great camaraderie.

I don't wish to sound preachy, but I worry for the young people and the intense scrutiny and judgement they are exposed to, even from themselves. I have been around fame long enough to know that you cannot fix what's broken and it can often make it worse. When fame is built on a solid bedrock of sound values, one can use it to do great things.

In all professions pertaining to the charlatans of today, you can fool some people some of the time, but not all the time. Thank God! In our industry worldwide, we still have passionate dancers who wish to achieve.

We have such wonderful talent and, as we know, it must be encouraged the right way and by people who themselves have accomplished.

Dancing to me is like breathing.

It holds a special fascination.

It is part of my heart and soul.

A means to express myself.

1968: What a year

The Dancers Club became of age. With humble beginnings, it was a great idea. However, through sponsorship from Mr. J. J. Shelly, the club had a new International Lounge built. On July 10th, 1968, it opened. Mr. Shelly was on the board of directors, as well as being president of the club itself. He was also the owner of Shelly's famous drink company. Alex Moore, M.B.E. from dancing, came from England for the opening.

The A.N.D.A held their championships at the Sydney Town Hall. The championships were commonly known as the Nationals. As part of the Championship competition, a team's event was included. Heats for the teams' event were held at The Dancers Club over a six-week period. Our team competed in many team heats to make the finals. With so many teams entering, the final six teams danced at the Sydney Town Hall as part of the competition on the day.

The team's event was called The Shelly's Shield Teams Match. The teams comprised four couples in grades - one in D grade, one in C grade, one in B grade and one A grade.

Our team was called The Reeve-ite Bush Bunnies. We even had a live bunny in a basket to carry onto the floor. I put my handbag in the basket for safekeeping and, needless to say, the lovely little bunny chewed it like nobody's business. It kept him quite occupied. All the teams' finalists had lovely team dresses and our dresses were a pale tangerine with a white sash. They looked lovely and we won! I was pregnant with my first child.

A short time after the Shelly's Shield, the F.A.T.D held their Professional Championships for Modern and Latin. We always had fun at this event. Darren New and Adele Fraser represented the studio at the Latin championships. They made the final and came second. At the championships we had our own allocated tables and we dressed our tables with the colour of Adele's Latin dress, which was black trimmed with hot pink. During the night, we had water pistols. Instead of filling them with water, we filled them with scotch. I really don't like scotch, I prefer brandy. It was a great night. It had to be seen to be appreciated.

Adele was also a great help in the studio at the time because of my pregnancy. Peter Todd was having a lesson when Ray received a phone call to go to Bulli Hospital, which was five minutes away. Donna was ready to be born. On September 20, Donna Monique Reeve came into the world. What a wonderful bundle of joy she was, and still is. Donna learnt to dance at minus six months. Who knew what a wonderful inclusion and happiness she would bring to Ray and me and later on to Dancing!

Everything was wonderful until six weeks later in October when the South Coast, Illawarra, was on fire. It was my first day back at work and Ray's mother was minding Donna at our home in Armagh Parade, Thirroul. We could literally hear the flames coming and exploding through the eucalyptus. Everyone said that the flames would not jump over Bulli Pass, but they did.

Ray went and got his mother and Donna from our house, grabbed our insurance policies, my white arctic fox fur coat and his tails, that were made in Savile Row, London - in the new shorter style. People asked why his tails? He said because they were for our work, which I thought (were) good thoughts.

Ray then took his mother home to the fire station, along with Donna, for safety. He then came and got me and we ventured up to our house. They barricaded all the roads off. The fire chief told Ray, "Not much use you going any further. Your house has gone."

However, being who he was, Ray broke through the barricade and kept going - lucky for us to find our house still standing. The flames jumped from the back of our house to the front. We were so unbelievably lucky. Only the house facia boards on the front were burning. Our good neighbours had torn off the torched facia boards with their bare hands.

Ray and our good friend John Minogue stayed on our roof all night. John was the Professional New Vogue Champion and also taught in our studio. There was not a single blade of grass left in our yard! To me, it resembled what the moon might have looked like.

We were invited to work on the Greek ocean liner, the *SS AUSTRALIS*, which was part of the Chandris Line. We would be demonstrating and teaching. We were part of the entertainment group. It was early December.

Ray and I couldn't sleep at night on board, thinking about our daughter Donna, who was staying with my sister Dawn. Until one becomes a parent, you can't explain the anguish for your children.

On one of our excursions, we went to a Fijian village. After drinking their kava and eating their honey cakes, they danced for us. We reciprocated by dancing the Cha-cha-cha for them. They loved it. When we left them, they sang for us. I cried. It was wonderful. The Fijians have the most beautiful voices.

The trip was successful. We had to join the Able Body Seaman Union when we returned to Sydney. When we collected Donna on our way home from the ship, she was as happy as ever, and very content. She was in good hands.

The greatest thing you'll ever learn,

is just to love

and be loved in return.

We were always improving

In our early days of competing, we attended the F.A.T.D. Ball championship event that was held at the Trocadero in Sydney. Tess Scully, the very famous ballet teacher, summoned us to her table after making her entrance surrounded by her entourage, which was about a mile long. She addressed us and said, "You should have won tonight, but you won't get it. Go home and practice for five years and no one will beat you." I was a little too young to understand her meaning, but she was so right. It takes that long for a partnership to mature. The young dancers of today do not have faith to work that long. With everything, it has to be now or yesterday.

Everything seemed to pay off. In 1964, The World Amateur Modern and Latin Championships were held in Sydney at the beautiful Town Hall. Australia had two couples in the Modern Grand Final. Kerry Wilson and his cousin Maureen Wilson, who were trained by us, ran fifth. The other couple were Dick Foley and Kay Waterman, trained by Henry Jacques and they ran 6th.

The results were England 1st and 2nd, Germany 3rd and 4th, Australia 5th and 6th. The only time that Australians placed again was in the grand final at The World Latin Amateur Championships held in Sydney, at The Hordern Pavilion, in 1972. Those results, particularly ours, have never been repeated by Australia.

1965 was a year of inspiration, both with our success and that of our pupils. It was of a very high standard.

In 1966, we won the South Pacific and Australasian in Brisbane. I can remember one Federal competition at The Trocadero in Sydney where we had six Amateur Latin Finalists and five out of the six Modern Finalists. Dick Foley and Kay Waterman at the time were reigning champions. So, Miss Kane decided to divide the dance floor and run two heats at the same time - for what reason, I do not know.

However, I thought this was not right. These wonderful couples deserved better. So, I told them to come off the floor and don't dance. Eileen accepted my decision and removed the rope that separated the floor. Eileen Kane said that they were all prima donnas, but I was the best one out of all of them. Incidentally, in the Modern, Kerry Wilson and Ann Harding beat the reigning champions, Dick Foley and Kay Waterman.

Many champions emerged. We were, at the time, triple undefeated Australasian and South Pacific Champions. During this time, we met more interesting and lovely people. One particular couple of international recognition were Maurice and Dolly Strowbridge from the UK. Maurice was a very fine photographer and Dolly was the best dancing dress and attire maker in the world.

We won the Australasian in 1966 and 1967, the latter being a huge year for us. We danced in Adelaide, South Australia for the Australasian. We did another tour of New Zealand and danced in The World Modern Championships in Melbourne, as well as the South Pacific Championships in Sydney. Prior to going to New Zealand in June of that year, I had a kidney operation. When I came out of hospital, I found it very hard to straighten up. Within two weeks, I was able to stand up straight, ready to dance.

We won The Australasian and South Pacific and were grand finalists at The World Championships. The World's had a semifinal, final and a grand final. After we danced in the final and came off the floor, I said that if we made the grand final, I didn't think I could go again and dance another round. We had done so much dancing.

However, when our number was announced for the grand final, we jumped up off the seat and all of a sudden, we had so much energy. It was a great reward for us.

Kerry Wilson and Ann Harding (source: Ann Harding-Trafford).

As always, the Australians had their eliminations on the same day as the grand finals. We had to dance two more rounds than the other countries who had already chosen their representatives from the Championships that were previously held in their own country.

The Asian Pacific Professional Championships were held at the same event. Kerry Wilson and Ann Harding won both of them! Much excitement for the studio.

It is hard work to get to the top of the mountain. The trouble is how to stay there? We achieved it! Not by politics, but by hard work, knowledge, talent and passion. The right place at the right time. It definitely was not for the money. We were Championship Teachers.

Everyone wants to succeed, but no one wants to prepare. Continuous effort, not strength or intelligence, is the key to unlocking your potential!

Believe in yourself and the rest will fall into place. Have faith in your own abilities. Work hard and there is nothing you cannot accomplish. Don't find fault, find a remedy.

Pertaining to dancing -

History, teaching and knowledge.

If I don't say something,

then I am agreeing with ignorance.

Further learning

We would've liked to have had the opportunity of staying longer in London 1965, when we represented Australia at The World Championships and danced in the British Open. We felt that we could have furthered our success by competing and learning even more. It was not to be. Our studio business, which had grown and was quite big, was beckoning us to come home. So, we did!

We looked at going again. We looked at all our priorities, but the costs involved were just too high. There wasn't any way we could contemplate it, though the desire was always there. So, in 1970 we approached The Chandris Line to employ us on The Australis again, and they accepted.

We worked our way over to England, going through the Panama Canal. It wasn't hard work at all. We did a show every second night and taught a one-hour class every second day.

During the shows, I had to perform Zorba's Dance with the ship's Greek Choreographer and Entertainment Director, Michael Charalambous. I loved to learn everything I could.

The captain loved our Cha-cha-cha and wanted to have some lessons. He summoned me to teach him in his cabin. I was a bit nervous. At sea, the captain is considered to be GOD. Ray to the rescue! The captain had a girlfriend on board and Ray suggested it would be a good idea if they learnt together, so they could dance together. The captain agreed to this and all was well.

The trip itself by boat was great, but it was not always easy for me. Travelling with us on this particular trip was our daughter Donna, who was 20 months old. The company was so good for us. They gave us a nurse to mind Donna while we did our shows. One night, Donna just wanted to be with us and wouldn't settle down. Ray picked her up as we did our encore bow, with Donna in his arms. She was quite content and lapped up all the attention. She was dressed in her little blue dressing gown and slippers.

Donna got quite sick on the boat and developed bronchitis. I think it was the air conditioning. That was the year we were introduced to disposable nappies - thank God! I also had to take baby bottles and a steriliser with me as well. When we arrived in England, she recovered greatly and had a wonderful appetite. Her love of food has never left her.

Prior to us leaving, we contacted our friends Dolly and Maurice about accommodation whilst staying in England. They introduced us to their friends, who were retirees and had a most beautiful home in a glorious position. He had been the editor of the English newspaper, The Sun. The address enhanced our accommodation - Melrose Gardens, Ashley Park, Walton-on-Thames, Surry.

We were among the rich and famous! In the same location we had living near us - Agatha Christie, Engelbert Humperdinck and The Beatles. Above all, the area was just beautiful.

We used to walk to the station each morning for fitness and it was just so lovely with the beautiful flowers, making a unique frame for all the uplifting flora of the homes.

Donna had such a great time playing with the squirrels in the parks and woods. Our hosts would take her there. By the way, this was the place where they filmed Robin Hood.

There was a gate to the Estate where we were living in Ashleigh Park. We would travel to London each day for lessons - to further our knowledge. After winning the Captain Cook Bicentenary Professional Championships earlier in the year, we had retired from competition as triple undefeated Professional Champions. We figured it was a nice title, seeing as we would not be around for the next centenary.

They looked after us so well at Ashley Park. At times, we would practice on the back lawn. Not to hurt it, of course. Donna wouldn't walk anywhere, so we bought a stroller and that solved the problem.

Staying in our house at Ashley Park was a young French student who used to entertain Donna. She taught Donna to play Baa-Baa Black Sheep on the piano. Not bad for 20 months.

We stayed in England for approximately 2 months. We learnt from the same teachers that we did when we were first there in 1965. Since that trip, we had kept in touch with them, forming wonderful friendships. To have lessons with the teachers, one had to book a year in advance. It took a lot of planning.

Our teachers in London were Len Scrivener, Nina Hunt, Bob Burgess, Doreen Freeman, Peter Eggleton, Brenda Winslade, Doris Lavelle, Sydney Francis, Michael Stylianos and Sonny Binick. Those teachers set standards in Ballroom Dancing and their theories and techniques still stand strong today. After Henry Jacques' teachings, our understanding of dancing became even stronger.

We were having a lesson with Len Scrivener one day and had to take Donna with us. Nellie Duggan, who was Len's partner, very kindly offered to mind Donna in their other room. Donna was dressed in a beautiful little pink playsuit. Everything went well as we finished our lesson with much appreciation for the babysitter. So, Nellie brought Donna out to us and, to our horror, she was covered in red Texta all over her suit and herself. No wonder she was having such a nice, quiet time.

We went sightseeing at Windsor Castle and I took a lovely photo of Donna and Ray on the castle steps, which I still have in one of our family albums. We also went to visit Hampton Court and took more photos. Every Christmas, when the family comes up for dinner, they drag all the family albums out. We reminisce about the wonderful times and memories that we shared as a family. The dance related photos are in our scrapbook.

Whilst working on the boat going over to England was great, it was very taxing with a baby, and we had had enough. We decided not to sail back home, opting for air travel instead.

Having decided to fly home from London, it was much easier for me pertaining to Donna. Travelling with Qantas, they were so good and thoughtful to us. They gave us an extra seat of three, plus a bassinet at the bulkhead for Donna.

We made a stopover in Singapore and stayed at the beautiful Raffles Hotel. One night, while having dinner at the hotel, Donna decided to do an impromptu dance on the stage. Up and away, she went with her dance routine at 20 months.

You don't have to be someone special

to achieve something amazing.

You just have to have a dream,

believe in yourself and work hard.

1972: A year like no other

When the time came around for the World Amateur Latin and Modern Championships, I knew that the international competitors wore special Latin suits. It was an all-in-one suit with a shirt underneath. We didn't have them. However, our larger-than-life friends Ray and Robbie Rivers came to the rescue.

Robbie borrowed Kerry Wilson's suit and made a pattern from it. Kerry had just returned from overseas and was up to date with the dress code. I was able to acquire the correct fabric - black ski suit material. Ray and Robbie made the Latin suits for our young men and they were so great.

So, in 1972, at The Hordern Pavilion in Sydney on October 7th and 8th, The World Amateur Modern and Latin, The Asian Pacific Modern and Latin and The Asian Pacific Professional Modern and Latin Championships were held. Three international events in NSW. Over 100 invitations were extended to over 60 countries who were represented on The International Council of Ballroom Dancing. They assured us that the World's leading competitors would attend.

We had three couples from our studio who did very well in The World Amateur Championships. Two of them made the Grand Final of the Latin. They were Doug Newton and Rosalyn Toulmin who placed 5th place and Greg Smith and Marion Alleyne who placed 6th. I knew these two successful couples were good enough to make the grand final - though they were not well known and I wasn't sure how they would be received. We also had one couple, just out of the Junior ranks, who made the 24 in the Latin. They were Peter Gerstenberg and Virginia Chesher.

In the Amateur Modern, John and Wendy Thornton who came down from Queensland to study, represented our studio and placed third in the final. They should have been placed higher because they danced great.

In the Professional Modern Asian Pacific, Kerry Wilson and Kerry Walker were first in the final, with Japan coming second. In the Latin they placed second in the final to Japan. What a great achievement for our couples. What a depth of great dancers we had and as a country we were very strong. They labeled our studio "the home of the champions."

Bobby Field, a dear friend and respected professional, said something to me after the competitions that I appreciated. "You are the only Australian teacher to have had couples with no overseas training in a World Grand Final and it will never be done again." It hasn't! I am a ten-dance teacher, which I just love.

Another couple, John and Carol Kimmins, came down from Queensland to train with us and then had gone to England to compete and study in 1971. They were lovely dancers who created a blazing a trail for our most talented. They came home and in 1975 won at the Australian Championships before returning to England in early 1976 and winning the British Amateur Open to The World. I think, with tongue in cheek, all those lovely Sunday afternoons at the famous Headlands Hotel helped in their preparation after their practice sessions.

Kerry Wilson and Kerry Walker, after returning home to us in Australia, migrated overseas to live in England. They represented Australia in Berlin at The World Professional Modern Championships in 1971 and made the Grand Final. Australia was lucky this time. They had an adjudicator at the event, who, incidentally, was Ray Reeve. The winners were Anthony and Fay Hurley.

John and Carol Kimmins.

John and Wendy Thornton.

A funny thing happened at that event. One of the English judges was out of order with his marks, so Ray, Anthony and Bill Irvine hung a black wreath on the door of his hotel room.

Kerry Wilson, John Thornton, Doug Newton and Greg Smith all went on to great success. Doug opened a very successful dance school in Wollongong, NSW. Greg and Marion went to England and stayed there. They still live overseas; Greg in the Netherlands and Marion in England. John Kimmins went to America. Carol eventually returned to Australia and opened up a successful studio. They all sprouted their wings nationally and internationally. I was and still am very proud of them.

Rounding off this wonderful month of dancing in October 1972 were The Australasian Championships, which had competitors from every state in Australia, including the ACT and New Zealand. We came back with several titles that year. The Championships were traditionally held in a different state each year. This year, it was held in Victoria. One month prior to the event, the S.A.T.D. ran their NSW selections. Each state, including New Zealand, also ran their own selections. All the state representatives would compete at the Australasian. Adding to the Australasian Championship event were other minor competitions, open to dancers who were not representatives.

The teams representing their states for The Australasian would travel to the host state fully sponsored by the S.A.T.D. for one week. The team representatives comprised the Professional, Amateur and Junior divisions in the three styles, Modern, Latin and New Vogue. We had such a great time with all the dancers staying together.

On one of our Australasian trips, all the teams were to travel together by train to Queensland. We were all under contract and no-one could break it.

We were on our way to Central Railway Station in Sydney. One of our pupils was driving us to the station when we were confronted by a huge traffic jam. Our pupil, Colin Gibson, said that we aren't going to make it in time. A big alarm!

Douglas Newton and Rosalyn Toulmin.

So, we improvised. There was a diesel engine parked at Waterfall Railway Station. Thank God for the NSW Government Railways. Ray and I hitched a ride on the diesel and I was wearing a white suit. However, it did the trick and got us there.

When we arrived at Central Station, one of the security guardsmen walked around with a megaphone letting people know where we were. "Ray and Margaret Reeve, last seen leaving Waterfall." So, they put us on another train and all was good. We made it but arrived later than our team. Given the circumstances, they gave us permission to dance.

Finishing 1972 were two more events. The first was the South Pacific, which was held in a different state each year. This year it was held in Sydney, NSW in November and run by the F.A.T.D. We came home with several titles.

The second, and last event of the year, was the Australian Championships, which were held in Melbourne. Again, we came back with many titles for our studio, including winning the Professional Titles in all three styles, the Amateur Modern and Latin. Some Junior couples also made the finals. This Australian was also very eventful for us in other ways. First, I couldn't attend as I was heavily pregnant. Our son Adam was born on December 6th. Second, there was a plane strike forcing some competitors to go earlier, travelling on their own, by bus or train to Victoria. Some of them even drove. Ray still had commitments at the studio, so he left later. Ray chartered a plane for himself and the rest of the studio competitors, approximately eight people in total.

Due to the high cost of chartering the plane, once the dancers had finished competing in their events, they had to return home via plane that same night. They had till 12.00 midnight to board, otherwise they would be left behind. They took no change of clothing, just what they had worn on the plane. As soon as their events finished, they quickly changed out of their dance attire, they took all their gear and headed for the plane.

Greg Smith and and Marion Alleyne (source: Marion Welsh).

What an amazing year 1972 was for dancing in Australia. International, national and state events, with competitors moving around the country weeks apart.

Those competitions and what the dancers had to work through in that year cemented for me what I always knew to be true. A dancer who does not understand how to have and use their presence can never be regarded to be an artist. Let me explain what I mean by that. One may be humble, but when they approach the dance floor, they need to step into the role of the competitor, ready to win. Whether they win or not is irrelevant. They should dance like they believe they win. Otherwise, their performance will fail to arouse interest or give enjoyment - THE X-Factor.

Practice every day and remember that interruption hinders progress and a loss never regained. Pertaining to dancing - worship beauty and never deviate from the true principles of your art. Above all, do not allow the temporary success of a few poor dancers, who please a blind public with their acrobatic antics, ridiculous lines and poor technique, lead you to emulate their errors.

The triumph of these worthless artists is of short duration. Egos! We should all have our own appearance and our own fame. Learn how to show your rhythmical feelings, emotional content with the correct technique and approach to the dance.

Truth and sincerity will find

the honest competitor in the end.

Showtime

In our infancy, we set a format for our studio Christmas party entertainment. We got our students together and they all would perform different acts. The Charleston, The Can Can, The Hula and even Swan Lake, which was a great success.

The boys' ballet danced Swan Lake. It was correct and very serious. The boys had tutus and ballet clothing. The most unlikely looking lot. We had a very talented ballet dancer who was learning ballroom with us, so she taught them their steps. It was so serious and everyone couldn't help but laugh. Many of our performers were our social dancers. As well as the acts for the show, we would provide supper. We had a small bar area set up where we would serve drinks that included our famous punch. There were also exhibitions from other couples as well. We had some marvelous shows.

So that our pupils knew how to dance well, we encouraged them to go for their medals. We taught them different basic routines for all the different grades. Bronze, Silver, Silver Bar and Gold as they advanced with sound training right up to the Gold Star Medal.

We then introduced our monthly, Sunday afternoon, dancing entertainment, POINT SCORE. It became very famous and known everywhere.

We had enough of our own couples to take part. The captains of the teams were our professional couples. We formed the structure of the competition with different coloured teams. Orange, green, blue and yellow and no one knew what team they were in until they drew their colour on the day. Each month, they had to draw for a team, so no one was ever in the same team twice.

Four teams competed and the point score comprised five sections plus an extra event where individual medalists without a partner were paired with an experienced amateur. At the end of the year, the couple who gained the most points received a fully paid return trip to Melbourne for The Australian Dancing Championships.

The point scores were great fun. We used them as practice each month for couples before they competed in Sydney and interstate events. Also, it was a way for new students without a partner, who wished to see what competitions were like, to participate. It gives them an opportunity to perform without a huge monetary outlay.

The winning team all received a beautiful large sash, but the most important thing was the competitive practice. Everyone was dressed in full attire to get them ready for their upcoming competitions.

We would eventually progress to the Woonona Bulli R.S.L. for our medal tests combined with our point score. We would conduct our point score sections between each medal test. As this venue was bigger, many parents, family and friends would attend and would make a day of it. They could then have dinner at the club, a glass of wine, whilst enjoying the show.

At The Woonona Bulli R.S.L, we ran a club show and it was open to all dancers., not only to our own couples, but to competition dancers from other studios throughout the state. The same format over six weeks. It was a Saturday night Amateur competition that was adjudicated, as well as having a demonstrating couple. Grand final night was so good.

We were never frightened of work. We loved our profession. One night we were demonstrating at the Fraternity Club to raise money for our 1965 trip to England. As we finished our show, the manager from the Piccadilly Night Club telephoned the Fraternity Club. He asked if we could go to his club and demonstrate, as his scheduled act hadn't turned up. Already dressed, we drove into

Wollongong from Fairy Meadow, ran up the stairs and put on our Latin show on a floor about as big as a ten-cent piece. All went well, though.

Speaking of clubs, one type of show that we ran for years was our club competitions. We would run these in many of our local clubs in the Wollongong area. We rang every club we could and there were so many of them. We wanted to promote our dancing and our students, and to see if the clubs were interested. It was a way for us to showcase Ballroom Dancing in the area and bring money into the clubs.

Our studio performed at - The Wollongong Workers Club, Thirroul Leagues Club, Thirroul R.S.L, Fraternity Bowling Club, Northern Suburbs Leagues Club, Corrimal Leagues Club, Dapto Leagues Club, Illawarra Yacht Club, Western Suburbs Leagues Club and the AGA Club Germania. Year after year, we would run these club shows. Some of these clubs are no longer with us.

The club shows played an important role in getting our studio name out into the community. It allowed us to extend our dancing business outside the studio walls. It also gave our students and competitive dancers the opportunity to enhance their performance skills and bring the joy of entertainment to the public.

Whilst we performed at many clubs, one club stood out for us and that was The Fraternity Bowling Club at Fairy Meadow. On the 29th August, 1953, the club was officially opened. A group of local Italians worked hard and pooled their money to get the club up and running. They wanted a place where the Italian community could come together. That same year, Ray started our first studio.

We ran our Latin Extravaganza at The Fraternity Club, very successfully, for almost fifty years. It was a six-week event. We held it approximately the same time every year, comprising heats, semifinals and grand finals. Each night was packed, but the Grand Final night was just something else. Everybody loved dancing for us at The Fraternity Club. Ray and I compared the show. Each week, we would have a professional demonstration and then the competitors. During these events, patrons used to have a wager between themselves on the couples. Our Professional demonstration couples comprised NSW, Australian, World and British Champions. The calibre of dancing was electrifying.

We gave out prizes from 1st to 6th place in three graded competitions, as well as the Open Grand Finals. The finals comprised six couples in each. They all received such wonderful gifts.

The Italians loved their dancing and they were very receptive. Being an Italian club, most of the audience was of Italian origin. Lots of clubs in the area operated and included Ballroom and Latin American competitive dancing, but none of them received the acclamation and appreciation like The Fraternity Club. Ray and I used to demonstrate there every year on New Year's Eve.

We all danced to a most wonderful Italian-Latin band called Con and The Latin Beats. The music was so exciting. Con was the most beautiful person. This would become one of the big highlights of my life, for the demonstrations that we did and the comparison of our own shows at the club. What a great time I had! So many opportunities to live my life to the fullest. After all, that's what life is all about. I've been having a blast of the recognition of the fun and enjoyment we all had. It was just like one big family.

Con's favourite dance was the Paso Doble, the dance of the bullfight. The crowd would go crazy about it. Our children danced there with their partners, first as amateurs and when they turned professional, they entertained us with their demonstrations. Ray and Judy Rivers also came down and demonstrated for us. We shared a great rapport as friends and still do.

Clive Phillips and Karen Phillips

I can never say enough about the fabulous Fraternity Club in a lovely way. Full of entertainment, learning and respect. Our shows were always alive and we always looked forward to that time of the year. After the heat was over for the night, we stayed on and danced the rest of the night to this wonderful band. It was so entertaining and exciting. People still ask if we are going to have our Latin Extravaganza again because of how many years we ran the show. So many still remember.

Con would always walk us out when we were finished and had to go. I have never met anyone enjoy life like he did. He was infectious. After Con died, the band was still good. He had left them his legacy.

I always loved promoting! I was never one to shy away from it. It became a great tool, as the studio would become known throughout the community. In the late sixties, a very well-respected man from our local area - in fact, he was Rosalyn Smith's father, Bill Toulmin. Bill helped to organise the Wollongong Eisteddfod. By that time, the Wollongong Eisteddfod had already been running for over 50 years. Encouraging young performers to showcase their talents in the arts, to dream and reach for the stars.

Bill and his wife, Phyllis, were a beautiful couple. Bill was so quiet, but a very strong, respectful man. Phyllis lived life to the fullest. Much to the entertainment at one of our get togethers after a championship at Canberra, run by Gwen Wallace, Mr. and Mrs Touilman came into the room. Kerry Wilson, who had a great sense of humour, said, "Here comes Wild Bill and Phyllis Diller." They were nothing alike, which added to the humour. There is a show on TV called Wild Bill, which reminded me of the incident. I think Rosalyn had a distinguished career dancing with four great partners.

Bill Toulmin suggested it would be nice to include Ballroom Dancing in the curriculum. He sought our advice and learned how to run an event. Thus the "South Coast Ballroom Dancing Extravaganza" was born. We ran this competition shortly after the Eisteddfod events had concluded. That way, it was still fresh in the air for Wollongong and it made a lovely ending.

This was a new venture for us. Only pre-registered entries were allowed. There were no entries on the day of the competition. We ran The Extravaganza in an old dance studio, which was not being used. Incidentally, my daughter Donna and her husband Alan moved the studio there as the first Dance Space 383 studio in Wollongong, following their move from Woonona. It was the perfect location as it was very close to the Wollongong Town Hall, which was in the CBD and home to the Eisteddfod.

The competition was only a small one, but so enjoyable. It grew each year. The Extravaganza became a huge success. We ran the

Extravaganza for approximately ten years at this venue, but we were bursting at the seams.

In 1965, they had finished work on the restoration of the Town Hall. To commemorate the newly restored Town Hall, they held a Civic Ball. Following the success of our early Extravaganza events, Ray and I were invited as guests to perform. We had opened the event with our dancing show. We were fortunate to have had Jim Gussey's ABC Sydney Dance Band. They provided wonderful music for the evening. We went in earlier that day to have a rehearsal with the band as well.

Our Extravaganza event eventually become "The South Coast Ballroom Dancing Spectacular" and we moved it to The Wollongong Town Hall. We filled it with such great memories. The Town Hall seats 600 people and often we had crowds of up to 1000. There was standing room only. As the years went on, our magnificent event had additions. Floor Shows from Professionals of the highest ranks.

One year, a very good Russian couple was here on holiday in Sydney. They contacted us and we engaged them to do a show at the competition. Well, in my excitement, I contacted our local newspaper The Mercury, and we got a first page coverage with my idea for the headlines. THE RUSSIANS ARE COMING.

The Town Hall was packed. Spectators came from everywhere to see. Not a seat left in the hall. We had, which would become a trend, our senior spectators sitting on the stage on chairs so they could watch the event in comfort. Approximately thirty of our seniors sat there. They loved sitting there. They felt important, as they truly had the best seats in the house. Each year, I would accommodate them. It was such a treat for them and for us.

This year, before our Town Hall competition, the manager of Cleo's nightclub approached us to run a Latin competition on a Thursday night for six weeks. Not a great night to run a show in Wollongong, but we did it anyway. The manager was most generous.

Each week, we allotted the winner of the heat $100 cash plus dinner for two. We had permission to call our show at Cleo's nightclub, THE LEISURE COAST LATIN EXTRAVAGANZA.

We filled the club each week. On Grand Final night, we had a hiccup. Our demonstrating couple was coming down from Sydney to perform but were running late. We had to go on and we couldn't keep the crowd waiting any longer. The last dance of the Amateur Competition ended and low and behold, our demonstrating couple ran through the door, and I might add, fully dressed in their dance costumes. They got changed in the car on the way down. They ran in and jumped on the stage. I got the gentleman organising the music to start their first dance - The Cha-Cha-Cha and they started their act. I announced to the audience that this was how we planned it. Beautiful dancers, Clive and Karen Phillips, Australian Modern Amateur Champions.

The following Sunday at the Wollongong Town Hall, we held The South Coast Ballroom Dancing Spectacular, where the Russian couple demonstrated for us. Whew, what a month!

We came up with a great idea in the way of a championship event and we called it TRIBUTE TO THE DANCERS. Our colleagues joined in to help us run it. We had a heat in Queensland run by Ray Rivers, another in Blacktown run by Barry Wall and Wollongong was run by us. The Federal Association also ran a heat in their yearly June competition. Canberra had one too, run by Gwen Wallace and lastly Melbourne held their event at The Medalist Travel Club. The winner of each heat in their respective State events would dance the Grand Final at The Woonona Bulli R.S.L. The winners of each heat received $100 prize money and the winner of the Grand Final received the ultimate prize - a return trip to The British Open to The World Championships, held in England. We advertised it as THE PRIZE OF THE YEAR. We ran this event for several years.

Promotions through our competitions also gave tribute to some of the great professionals from back in the day and their contribution to the arts. The problem was, we ran out of professional couples. However, we took those tribute prizes and gave them to the Amateurs at our South Coast Ballroom Spectacular.

We still run this competition, and then a lovely thing happened. There was a magnificent ballroom in Thirroul getting built and I had a meeting with the owner just as they began construction. I could see the potential. Straight away, I knew this venue would be perfect for our competition. I booked it for the next five years. The magnificent Anita's Theatre, built by the owner, who dedicated it to his late wife.

Now becoming one of the most popular events of the year, The South Coast Ballroom Dancing Spectacular has been running for sixty years. Not only is it popular with the local community, but the dancing community as well. We even had some overseas couples come to compete. They would stay and have lessons with us at the studio, making it worthwhile for them. We ran our competition differently to how others ran theirs. We wanted to make it fun as well as encouraging for the dancers too.

> ***Great dancers are not great***
>
> ***because of their technique.***
>
> ***They are great***
>
> ***because of their passion.***

Celebrities and showbiz

This chapter talks about some of the diverse things that we did with our shows and demonstrations. Because of our successes and public attraction, often after doing a show, we would get booked again for another one.

In the early 1960s ABC TV ran a wonderful series called TV BALLROOM. Ray and I were given the first production number for the series. Our demonstration number was set to a beautiful piece of music called Clair de Lune by French composer Claude Debussy. We had to have ballet lessons.

The sequence was Ray, looking at my photograph on top of the piano he was playing, intermittently while he was smoking a cigarette. They had a huge smoke machine and I came in dancing out of the mist and we performed our act. At the end of our dance, the story told Ray walking back to the piano and continuing to smoke his cigarette as I danced away back into the mist, whilst Ray stared at my photograph. We absolutely loved dancing and acting every minute of it. It was a huge national ABC TV production.

During the TV series, they held a competition. We came first and our very good friends, Kevin Calderon and June Bratt, came second. Alf Davies was the sole adjudicator and, funnily enough, he was also Kevin and June's coach. That just goes to show the honesty and unbiased opinion of the adjudicator. This was a wonderful win for us - on national television for the whole of Australia to see.

In the second TV Ballroom show, teachers could nominate one of their students to dance with. Kerry Wilson was our best dancer and pupil. Ray thought I should dance with Kerry. So, I did and we won!

There was also a team match competition. Teams representing their studio. So much hustle and bustle. We raised the money and whipped up four lovely dresses for the girls on the team. We even had the boys (much to our regret) help with the sewing of the sequins onto the lovely white dresses decorated in silver and royal blue. Our regret using the boys to help decorate the dresses was that they tried too hard to sew on the sequins rather shockingly, so that way, we would ask them to forget about it.

They looked so nice, but the show's director, George Trevare, kept changing the space that we were expected to dance on, because they wanted the camera to pick it all up. It was such a huge floor, but he wanted to condense it. As a result, the dresses kept getting caught on each other because the space was so tight. We expressed our concern with what was happening, but our expectations fell on deaf ears.

So, Ray said, "Okay guys, they're not serious here, we are going home." Trevare said, "You can't do that, we have a show." Ray said, "Yes we can, just watch us." So, the director compromised and gave us more room. Thus, a good performance was delivered with a much-deserved win too.

Each time, during the rehearsals, George Trevare would address the audience and the performers with his back to the stage. Ray and Kevin Gibson - who was up from Melbourne for his and Shirley's show - would link arms and dance ballet coupes across the stage.

The audience loved it and they all laughed, unbeknown to George. He was so bewildered when he turned around to look at the stage, there was nothing going on. The Reeve/Gibson ballet wasn't performing at that time. This performance happened about three times in all and I don't think George was any the wiser. After that, we trained with Alf Davies and with great respect. We became the best of friends and we had such a great rapport.

Alf Davies and Julie Reaby had not long returned from England. We thought that because they had won the British Championship, Alf must know something, having all that training and a successful time in England to achieve the ultimate prize. His unbiased opinion was always well received. As well as training with Alf and Julie, our coach at the time was Charles Froulop. Charles was a lovely man, such a gentleman, and so we had two coaches.

Alf and Julie came down for lunch one Sunday and Julie and I discussed my dresses. Hence, with her advice, my white feathered dress was born. Julie suggested putting feathers around the bottom of my ballroom dress. I had never heard of that before, so I had to figure out a way to do it. I was the first ballroom dancer that I know of, to have feathers on my dress, which I made myself. That dress has been copied many times by others since then. The feathers being soft and flowing added to the movement of the dress.

The ABC TV Ballroom series was great for dancing. We had a great rapport with our TV Stations. There was always a show to do. One such show was The Mike Walsh Show and it was so popular. The Mike Walsh Show was always on at midday and eventually the show would become The Midday Show. Everyone watched it. He was a great host.

We just loved doing shows. We also danced on the Don Lane Show several times. Bert Newton was on the show as well. He was so lovely to us. On one show with Susie Elelman from Win 4 in Wollongong, Bert even mentioned us. "How's Ray and Margaret? I haven't seen them for a while, great dancers." This was pertaining to us, living in the Wollongong area. He never forgot us and it was sad to learn of his passing.

During our heydays, along with our pupils, we ran a six-week dance show on WIN TV (Channel 4) showing every style of dance. It was called DANCING THROUGH THE AGES. We even did the BLACK BOTTOM, which was a dance from the 1920s, and one week we danced as Beatnik's to Dave Brubeck's tune Take 5. A very famous bohemian number.

Peter Allen came to town and the first show we did was on the same bill as him, at the Wollongong Diggers Club. He appeared with another man as part of a duo and they called themselves The Allen Brothers. After that, we did a few more shows with them on the same bill. He was lovely.

Peter wrote songs that the whole world sang and fronted a few of them himself. From I GO TO RIO to the deeply personal TENTERFIELD SADDLER. Despite his international success, his voice is synonymous with Australia, thanks to his unforgettable song, I STILL CALL AUSTRALIA HOME.

Watching the 2015 two-part miniseries, Not the boy next door, the story about his life, brought back lovely memories. He was such a great entertainer and had worldwide acclaim. He was so rhythmical and innovative.

In 1971, they invited Ray and I to give an exhibition at The Festival of Perth. The Festival of Perth was organised by Mr. Sam Gilkison, of the very famous Gilkison family, in the ballroom industry. We performed in a Ballroom Pageant as demonstrators. To our delight, we were on the same billing as Count Basie, one of my favourite jazz artists. We were so honoured to do so.

I have had many highlights in my career. A lovely one was in 2004 when I was invited to Tokyo to The Prince Mikasa Cup, to adjudicate. Adam and Karen Reeve were part of the top professional couples that were demonstrating and I was introduced onto the floor to meet my son Adam and his lovely wife Karen, who won the 2003 World Professional Ten Dance Championship in Japan the year before. Adam is the only Australian to win a Professional World 10 Dance Championship.

My life has never been dull. I won the inaugural Modern and Latin Brolga awards for coach of the year from the A.D.S. Then after that, I won the Brolga award for Latin, four more times.

We were honoured by (N.I.D.A.) the National Institute of Dramatic Arts, for our contribution to the art of Ballroom Dancing. Tongue in cheek, I used to say that we should have called our studio NIDA, as I would often refer to our students as great actors!

From our successes, I was fortunate to have been invited to judge quite a few World Ballroom Dancing events. The World Latin Championships in Munich, The World Professional 10 Dance Championships in the Netherlands, The World Professional Modern Championships in Hungary and The World Amateur Modern Championships in Australia. I felt exhilarated to judge these world events. I was also very nervous, but so glad for the experience.

One of the loveliest times for me was the meeting of Li Cunxin, one of the most beautiful ballet dancers in the world. Famous for the movie and true story called MAO'S LAST DANCER. I was so thrilled. I met him again at The Australian Championships in Melbourne and he remembered me.

He is now retired and I recently saw him on a TV commercial for A.P.I.A. insurance. He is still fantastic. After retiring from performing, he returned to dancing and in 2012 became the Artistic Director of Queensland Ballet.

"Dancing in all forms cannot be excluded from the curriculum of noble education" - Pierre Dulaine. Pierre would say these wise words, that were part of a quote by famous German philosopher Friedrich Nietzsche. In 2006, a movie called Take the Lead, starring Antonio Banderas, was released. It was the story of a New York dance teacher and former competitor who volunteered his time to teach a diverse group of school students. This is the story of Pierre Dulaine.

In 1994, Pierre founded Dancing Classrooms, a school dancing program aimed at teaching students to dance, as well as helping them with their social skills, confidence and awareness. The program became so popular it became integrated as part of the curriculum in New York Schools and throughout the USA. It is still running.

In 1972 Pierre was asked to be the cruise director by the Chandris Lines on their ship Amerikanis, a position that he accepted. The Amerikanis sailed from New York to the Caribbean. Incidentally, the Chandris Line was the same cruise line that employed Ray and I in 1968 & 1972. Pierre, with his partner Yvonne Marceau, won the British Exhibition Professional Championships four times. 1977 - 1979 and again in 1982.

Several years ago, Adele Hyland brought Pierre Dulaine down to Stanwell Park, on the South Coast - a delightful spot to have lunch with Alan and Donna. Luckily, the children had half a day off school, so Donna was able to bring them to lunch as well. Much to Donna's delight, they met Pierre and he did a cha-cha-cha with Frejya, then Charley and Frejya did one together for him.

It was a memorable event for them to see Pierre again. He had been so exciting during his career. Everyone loves him for his knowledge, love of dance and great knowledge.

From ballroom dancing to cricket. I always watched the cricket to see one of our local greats - Dennis Lillie. I absolutely loved him so much. One of my students, Brett Dorney, acquired an enormous poster signed by him. It was the same year I won the inaugural Brolga Award. *To Dear Margaret - Keep Up The Good Work*. I still have that poster. Baz Luhrmann did the same thing with a lovely autographed poster of Strictly Ballroom.

Whether we were just demonstrating or part of a bigger production, Ray was very particular and made sure that we were always well rehearsed. Ray and I demonstrated in nearly every club on the South Coast. We also performed at other events throughout

NSW and Canberra. As we used to say, "We were frequently employed." We never refused a booking!

Believe in yourself and the rest will fall into place. Have faith in your own abilities. Work hard and there is nothing you can't accomplish.

Lectures and Campsie

When we first came home from England in 1965, we had the pleasure of lecturing for the F.A.T.D. The lecture was open to everyone.

One of our lovely and prestigious professionals, Mrs Jacques, attended our lecture. We were so delighted to have someone of her credibility come to hear us. Her comment she made about the Australian Professionals was, "They won't believe what you have to say, they won't comprehend and they won't want to do it."

The professionals did not want to learn the basic concepts, but they wanted to learn all the modern choreography. Just like that song "It don't mean a thing if it ain't got that swing." Which meant, if you didn't understand the technique of swing, sway, rise and fall, it didn't matter what you did. We did many lectures for the associations and the dancing fraternity in each state of Australia, including Canberra.

Lectures weren't organised every week, but wherever we taught, they would ask us to give a lecture. Ray and I in Modern and myself in Latin. People loved my isometric exercises. These exercises helped the students with their flexibility and the use of their body rhythm to our Latin American rhythms/modern music.

I always taught we had foot rhythm and body rhythm. One is no good without the other. The overall competitive package has to include the lot.

We had a small child in our studio who was learning to dance Modern. She already learnt tap and ballet. She was eight years of age and very good. One day, she was pulling faces when I walked past her and I said, "Why are you pulling faces"? Her answer was - she was practicing her face dancing. I thought, how wonderful.

When we dance, we have so much feeling inside, but we don't always show it. One great exponent of the Latin Style, who had no problem expressing his facial feelings and who is a very dear friend of mine, is Espen Salsberg. What a great dancer. He had everything to enjoy watching.

Our lectures became well known. Not only did we lecture around Australia, but we lectured many times in New Zealand, Hong Kong and Taiwan. In Taiwan, the students did not speak English and I did not speak Chinese. It wasn't easy, however. Donna and Paul helped me out by being my demonstrating couple, and I had an interpreter. It was like playing charades, but I got through it and then I carried on with my teaching to explain that, "Face dancing was very helpful."

Hong Kong was different. It was much easier. I was taken to Colin Pople's studio. He wanted to do medal tests at the studio in Hong Kong, as there were no medal tests done there at the time. I lectured there for four consecutive years and sometimes the same students would come along. I would lecture, teach and examine. Colin was such a great host, a lovely dancer and a great competitor. It was tiring, but the pupils hung onto every word. They wanted to learn so much. In our lectures, we would talk about kinetics. We must not dance with physical strength. Hence, Henry Jacques teachings. *Minimum effort for maximum effect*. Many people, even to this day, don't understand.

We had a great formula for our lectures - balance plus control and how to use them. Explaining how one can exercise movement from a controlled base. The standing leg moves the moving leg and the moving leg moves the body. Theories of rise and fall were definitely one of our big subjects. We wanted so much to impart the knowledge that we had encountered and we were in great demand.

When I started to learn Latin American, there were no theory books. The learning curve involved writing the knowledge and theory in a notebook after having a lesson with your teacher. George Weiss, a dance teacher from NSW, as well as the head of the BDA (British

Dance Association) in Australia, paid for this English lady, Miss Gladys Ede, to come out from England to teach here in Australia. Her principles were so good and helped the Cuban Rumba along - dancing on the second beat. Previously, we danced the square or box rumba on the one. This Cuban beat was much more exciting. She also taught me the exact positioning of the toes and heels of the footwork in the Viennese waltz.

Doris Lavelle also came to Australia to teach and to lecture. We had Doris as one of our Latin teachers whilst we were in the United Kingdom. Ray Rivers prepared us for our Latin style to represent in The World's and The British Championships in London.

Doris had this wonderful little French guy in her studio and when we attended her class. I used to dance Jive with him. He was a star. I also had Latin lessons with Enyd Connelly in Australia, and to this day, I and the studio still use her medal routines. I found them to be the best constructed. I loved all my lessons. I have always enjoyed the Latin rhythms and having gained a lovely adaptation of the learnings and the musicality; it led to a whole new interpretation for my teaching and motivation.

One year while teaching in Melbourne, at Neil Rosenfeld's studio, Ray was explaining to a couple how the body swings up through the use of the standing leg. He explained how a ball compresses against the floor before rising and was pretending to bounce the ball while Ray Rivers and Neil pretended to be the Harlem Globetrotters bouncing the basketball and singing their song SWEET GEORGIA BROWN, making fun of Ray. Ray then said, "That's why the Globetrotters were so good, because they understood the swinging up of their bodies from a compressed position." We must always swing up, never down.

Another highlight of my life was when Mrs Jacques asked if I would give her Latin lessons. I was truly honoured. Doug Henderson, who was an old friend of Mrs Jacques and her husband Henry, would drive her down to our Thirroul studio.

Donna, who was four at the time, would often hear us talk about Henry Jacques. She thought that Doug Henderson was Henry Jacques and so she would say, "Hello Mrs Jacques, Hello Mr. Jacques". We taught her to say "Hello Mrs Jacques", but she took it upon herself to say, "Hello Mr. Jacques". It certainly was a delightful time. Mrs. Jacques was the most beautiful person.

Doug Henderson, who was a New Zealander, returned to his home country and Mrs Jacques continued out her days with her children. A lovely time shared.

Around 1971-1972 we arranged to take over the Jacques` studio in Campsie. Mrs Jacques had had enough by then and she asked us to take it over. Ray would go up to teach two nights per week and Kerry Wilson on the other nights.

Michael and Vicky Barr taught lessons in the Campsie studio as well. Michael and Vicky were a British championship couple who were here in Australia for several weeks. We asked them if they would be interested in teaching some classes at Campsie. We were so pleased to have them. They were such great teachers and lovely people - very professional.

It was quite a profitable little business. However, to our dismay, the city council pulled down all the shops (including the Campsie studio) in that block, to modernize the area. So, we thought it best to finish our trading there. The students from Campsie were so enthusiastic. Many of them followed us down to our Thirroul studio.

As I have mentioned many times, we have had the great fortune of meeting so many lovely people and we have met - as in every competitive industry - some were not so nice.

I just love quality.

Quality can be so broad.

It is available to all of us.

The glamour and the friendships

My very first competition was an amateur event at the Surreyville Dance Hall, Darlington, NSW. It was a large venue and to see such glamorous gowns all twirling around the dance floor was just so exciting. The Surreyville Dance Hall dates back to pre-1900 as a place of gatherings, assemblies, and, of course, the dance nights. Dance bands performed with couples young and old dancing the night away. It was extremely popular in the 1950s, and dances were run frequently. It was situated opposite the Sydney University and the once frequented department store Grace Bros. Eventually, the Surreyville Dance Hall would become home to The Bodenwieser Ballet for many years, and is now an acting hub.

My first Professional Championships dancing with Ray was at Sydney Town Hall. It was such a great atmosphere and we came third. We were thrilled; it was so exciting. The Sydney Town Hall is a magnificent heritage listed building built from local Sydney sandstone. It would also become home to The South Pacific Championships when it permanently moved to NSW. before moving again to Homebush. The N.S.W branch of The Australian Dancing Society also held their Championships at Sydney Town Hall. Its decor is beautifully ornate with a grand staircase that has marble treads. Such a glamorous venue and one of my favourites. The floor was so beautiful to dance on - it was all sprung.

I think my most favourite venue, at the time, was the ballroom at The Southern Cross Hotel, in Melbourne. The combination of glamour and decor made one feel special. The first time we stayed at the Southern Cross Hotel was in 1962, when The World Championships were held at Festival Hall. Later, the Medalllst Travel Club would run their glamorous competition, The Southern Cross Ballroom Championships at the hotel. The ballroom would also hold many prestigious and black-tie events. On entering the ballroom, a wall of mirrors decorated by beautiful lighting greeted guests. Not only was it stunning, it was enormous and the running of the Championship was quite spectacular. That era of dancing and fashion was so enjoyable to be part of.

I used to love going down to Melbourne for those Championships. I would meet up with my friends and we would have a great time. Even though we were all competitive, we never spoke to each other about our couples. We felt we didn't need to, as we were all very successful dancers and good teachers. We would just talk about everyday events and our experiences with the administration of dancing.

We all stayed in the hotel itself whilst the Championships were being held - such a beautiful hotel. Between the competition sessions, we would go up to our rooms and change into our evening and glitzy wear.

All the dancers would succumb to temptation and stay at the hotel. It was packed! One found it very hard to get the lift when needed. We really needed this time between sessions to get back to the ballroom for the adjudicating. So, making a remarkable discovery, I found a lift for room service and it was operating empty. We used it to solve our dilemma. Otherwise, we would have been waiting and we would have been late.

In 1965, Ray and I danced at the Winter Gardens, Blackpool, home to the British Championships, which I thought was the ultimate venue. I have never, in all my life, seen such ornate decoration and architecture. It was and still is beautiful. The venue had three tiers of seating. The first tier had seating in the boxes and it went all around the room. It was fabulous for viewing, with two bars for refreshments on the floor.

At the British Championships, a visitor could only gain a seat in the front row if they had won the British Championship title or adjudicated in one. Alan Shingler has done both - most prestigious. One year he took his daughter (my granddaughter) Freyja to visit her other grandparents and to see the Winter Gardens ballroom. Freyja sat in her father's seat in the front row. He was very proud of her and everyone loved her.

One of the other venues that I loved to go to and still do is the Crown Entertainment Complex in Melbourne, where you would also find the Crown Casino. The Crown Championships are held there and differ from other Championships. There were two ballrooms divided by a mirrored concertina wall. They not only had a ballroom competition running, but were simultaneously running a jazz and hip-hop competition in the other ballroom. Upon entry, a winding staircase leading up to a beautiful foyer into the ballrooms greeted you. Such class and glamour. Hopefully, it will continue to operate after the Covid 19 situation.

Another beautifully decorated Art Deco theatre is the Anita's Theatre in my hometown. Dripping chandeliers decorated in gold were everywhere, even in the restroom. We ran many wonderful competitions there. It was a true glamour ridden ballroom.

These particular venues were my favourites. I simply loved the glamour these promotions offered to us. True venues to enjoy our lovely dancing. Of course, there were other lovely venues we danced in all over the world, but none as nice, glamorous, or full of atmosphere as my favourites.

We always dressed very smartly when attending our lessons and practice, and it didn't stop there. I would often come home from work and finish making a dress that was half done to wear to practice that night.

With André, my first serious partner, everything had to look just right to be part of our glamorous art. I still think of dancing as an art, not a sport. One has to be good, but also fit to show the adjudicators how good you are. Everything was all very correct and part of an enjoyable, glamorous era. We were not governed by the rules and regulations that are in place now. We had more freedom in our teaching. It was all good, though I must say, not politically correct.

Charles Leasing, a teacher from Melbourne, was an older gentleman who had such charisma. He was one of the loveliest friends I had. He loved our teaching and he loved our pupils. We would never stop laughing at some mishaps that happened on the floor with our students. He commented that, even though you could tell the students were trained by me, they all were different and they all had their own character. He was such a gentleman.

Our other group of friends in NSW were Peter Kelly, Jan Blanch, Ray and Judy Rivers, Kevin Calderon and June Bratt, The Penelope Cay Studio and Enyd Connelly. Our bond was something else. The fun, entertainment and rapport were the foundations of our great friendship that has never been lost. A lot of these friends have passed now, hence the three Rs were born: Ray Reeve, Ray Rivers and Neil Rosenfeld. To this day, we are still in contact with each other - such good friends. We all knew how to laugh and enjoy ourselves.

At one of the South Pacific Championships that Federal had arranged, they gave us meal vouchers. The vouchers were to be used for food, or an occasional fruit juice, drink or coffee. Well, the venue was very crowded and Brian Duncan, one of our committee members, had the job of handing out the vouchers to us Judges. He was a very nice and helpful young man. Brian was a wonderful friend and a great help to Bob and Leigh Steele at the Federal Association. However, during the night session, I somehow accumulated quite a number of meal vouchers. So as not to lose them, I stored them down my dress front in my bra. I didn't want to waste them, so I gave them out to my fellow professionals. Funny thing was, my pupils that were sitting down could see me handing them out, pulling them out of my bra one at a time. They were all hysterical. It was the best South Pacific Championships I have ever been to - so happy and enjoyable.

These friends were special - a group of people who were always there for each other. Our life was dancing. We danced in glamorous ballrooms with style and elegance. Our friendships kept us grounded and we knew how important they were - we appreciated each other!

Dancing is one of the world's favourite pastimes.

Mostly enjoyed by everyone.

The best reason to embrace sharing.

Threats

I was once asked if we had ever been threatened. Well, yes, we had - a few times. I think that our success and that of our children was just too much for some people, so they turned their frustrations into threats - all anonymously, of course!

One of our very nice Latin champions from the earlier years, Colin Hilary, wrote a very interesting article that touched on this subject. It appeared in The Australian Dancing Times where Colin was also the editor. This magazine has been closed now for many years. Colin and his wife Joy moved to Florida in the USA and staged a most wonderful annual championship event called The Heritage Classic Ballroom Dancing Championships. It ran for many years and still does. Below is the article written by Colin Hilary, appearing in the 1968 July/August edition.

"Knockers" are "losers"

In the competitive field of dancing, it is comparatively easy and particularly interesting to observe the actions and reactions of individuals, especially in relation to their position on the competition ladder.

It's true there can be only one winner, but I have detected a pattern which usually depicts a "loser" and this is by their self-destroying habit of "knocking" practically everything that is better than they are capable of producing. (Incidentally, "knocking" has nothing to do with "bumping" into other couples on the floor).

It is not restricted to the active competitor by any means, but can be applied to anyone who has nothing of any value to contribute or is just too lazy to try. The habit apparently is very hard to break, for, once started, it quickly kills all initiative by removing incentive, making a comeback even harder. Confirmed addicts can be detected by their ability to justify a loss far easier than accepting normally any success they may stumble upon.

Australians generally tend to knock their own countrymen, and I wonder whether this has any bearing on our position in the world of ballroom dancing.

The Australasian Dancing Times is designed to promote you - the dancer, if you're worthy of it. So, ask yourself just one question - "What have I achieved and what am I contributing to the art of dancing?"

The first threat was when someone put tack nails under the tyres on our car. I had seen some small tacks on the ground when we came outside after the competition had finished, but I thought nothing of it. We were returning home after The South Pacific Championships at Homebush. Luckily, we discovered their appearance and made it home safely.

The next one was when Ray and I were coupled with dance teachers, Alex and Julie Schembri, in the form of a poster that had been sent out to all the major dance studios and associations in Australia. They were accusing us of using our friends in the dancing industry to mark/score our children favourably in competitions. This was quite a serious accusation, so we took it to the official board of Ballroom Dancing. We held a meeting with them and on their advice suggested that we hire a solicitor. Unfortunately, with no name on the poster, it stopped us from pursuing it any further.

Another time, a person posted a letter to me that I never knew about until just recently. (Ray had kept it away from me, as he considered it rubbish). The funny thing was that the person who sent the letter anonymously showed their intelligence by writing their name and address on the back of the envelope. Not very bright!

Then in the 1980s, another letter, another threat. These people, we had an idea who they were, threatened to break my daughter Donna's legs in the dressing room and put a bomb under our car. There definitely was some connection.

By then, trying to play this all down under the advice of our solicitor, Ray had had enough. One person was pretty game and came up to him at the end of a Federal Championship. He said, "Hello Mr. Reeve, are you still fixing comps?" Ray responded, "Yes and I'm pretty good at it."

One does not win a British or World Championship unless they really deserve it, and my children did. By the rules governed, as parents, we were not allowed to judge our children or relatives in competitions.

Following is an article written by Peter Smith that was published in the November 1994 edition of the Australian Dance Review. This article was a lead up to the reality of what happened to Ray and I and our children. It was one of the best articles I have ever read. It also best describes what these people were doing and had done with their devious actions. They did not know how hard it was, in any sport or art, to be top of one's game. It's a brilliant piece and puts to rest their cowardly attempts to try to derail us.

"Strictly Success"

In the almost twenty years I have been a member of the Dance Media, for lack of a better expression, it has been the policy of the two publications I have been seriously involved with - **Dance News**, *the World's leading weekly dancing publication from its origins in the United Kingdom, and the* **Australian Dance Review** *where I was the founding Editor - to file all anonymous correspondence where it rightly belongs - in the* **GARBAGE BIN!!**

However, this is one such piece that is currently doing the rounds, if only for its sheer downright libelous remarks, has coerced me to put pen to paper, or more truly to sit here at my word processor and punch the keys.

It appears that almost all members of the dance profession in Australia have found this most critical piece in their letter boxes in the last few days, sent with of all things a sender's address on the back of the envelope (which I am led to understand is fictitious). The enclosed flyer has some very damming reflections on all the professions, with particular emphasis on two very well-known dance teachers and their respective offspring.

All competitive sport is never without its dramas and all sports that fall into the category of being a "not first past the post" sports such as diving, gymnastics and of course dance sport, have and always will have more than their fair share of these. Think seriously for a moment and have a long hard look at the history of sport in general in almost every type of sport you can imagine, from tennis through all the football codes to horse racing. All over the world, the off-spring of former successful participants are currently becoming very successful themselves. Was not the horse of last Tuesday's Melbourne Cup trained by the son of a former great trainer? Is there not a son of a former Rugby League star currently on tour in the United Kingdom with the current Kangaroo Rugby League team and his dad was no less the Chairman of Selectors! Tut tut! Did his dad get all his mates on the selection panel to do him a favour and pick him for the touring party? Not likely! He simply was producing the goods and was selected on merit.

Now, to this diabolical piece, that is the point of my sitting here belting the buttons on this keyboard. Is there some relevance in the off-spring of dance teachers being successful in our field? Of course, the answer is a big YES. Without recourse to the obvious suggestions of bias and favoritism by the judging panels, just think about it. They have been brought up in a world of competitive dancing since the day they were born, their parents had a lot of talent and tenacity in their competitive careers and have passed this onto their children and on most occasions, they are simply the best in their respective grades on the day. If that means they take home the booty, so be it! If other couples want to beat them, then they must work hard, put in the hours' training necessary and get better than their opposition and then they will win regardless of whose kids they are dancing against. Believe me, it will happen.

No one is ever going to convince you or me that our system is perfect but the Skating System, devised by a very old and dear friend of mine - the late great Charles Jacobs - that is used worldwide for the collation of the judges' marks is as near as we are going to get to having the perfect system for dance sport and those that do not understand it should take the time to study it and learn its idiosyncrasies.

Now to the crux of this matter. Whoever you may be that went to the time, trouble and considerable expense to distribute this disgusting document all around Australia, please do yourself and all the rest of us a favour and do what I am about to do, have the guts to put your real name to it than your opinions will be at least respected by all of us and who knows, even some of your ideas and suggestions for a bigger and better world of dance may get to see the light of day.

In the meantime, I am off to give my daughter and her partner a lesson. So don't worry about the Reeve`s and the Schembri`s and their respective partners. Look out, the Smith`s are about.

Peter Smith

PS. The next time you write to us, please make sure you spell my wife's Christian name correctly - It is Rosalyn, not Rosalynd - she has a phobia about people spelling her name correctly.

Maybe for some people, they become so disappointed in what they are doing; they focus their attention on what they think others are doing, trying to bring them down in the hope it will make them feel better. Yet, with all the above mentioned, it fails compared to all the wonderful friends and acquaintances I have made through dancing.

One day, all of us will become separated from each other. We will miss our conversations. Days, months and years will pass until we really see each other again. Perhaps we should reflect on those moments. Moments that we cherished, with our friends and especially our families. On becoming a grandmother, I understood clearly that it doesn't make me old, it only makes me blessed.

One day, our children will see our photos and ask," Who are these people?" I will smile with invisible tears and say, "It was with them I had the best days of my life."

If you want to get it, you have to give it.

Respect is a two-way street!

Families

When I first began teaching at our studio, we had a family called the Robertsons, who would attend our Thursday night class. Mother, father and their three children all showed up to enjoy the night of social dancing, and they would come every week. They were such a lovely family and it really was wonderful to see how much they enjoyed it.

As the studio developed over time, we had siblings, cousins and even multiple siblings, all learning how to dance. They started out as students and many of them became competitors and so many of them became champions. How fantastic it was to have more than one champion in the family!

We also had students coming further regionally out of the local area, and some coming from interstate. Such was their dedication and commitment to their dancing. Some of these students would travel alone, or accompanied, some staying overnight or for the weekend, before returning home. We even had couples move to the area for their dancing. More recently, one such couple was Eric and Molly. Eric came from Melbourne and his partner, Molly, came from America. Such wonderful dancers and lovely, respectful people.

When one went to a dancing competition, it was the only way to see who your competitors were and the level that they were at. It was through those competitions that we and our students were noticed. We would often get approached to teach a student who lived quite a distance away or even out of state. Before long, entire families would move to our local area for their children to continue dancing at our studio.

We had the Jackson family - so talented. Brother and sister team Alan and Pam, who were Junior Champions. Kerry Wilson's parents and Rosalyn Smith's parents also came to the studio to dance socially on a Thursday night.

Graham Wilson and Caroline Paidasch.

The Oliver family came over from Perth to live and further their dancing. A daughter and three sons - Leslie, John, Ken and Russell. They all danced, were very competitive and their love of dancing was so strong. All had great success and results with their respective partners. Incidentally, the families are still living in the area.

Over time, names like the Price family would become well known. They had two sons who were both wonderful, successful dancers, and they soon would win titles. The Skeggs family were Lyndon and his sister Vicki, who both danced. The family moved down from Sydney. Lyndon would have a successful partnership with a local girl, Michelle Pincham. Other families were the Horrell, Fripp, Contreras, Mole and Whitehall families, just to name a few.

When I think about the earlier days of the studio, though, some families stood out for various reasons. We had two prominent families who came from Wagga Wagga, and I assure you that ALL the children from both those families became champions or finalists in the Australian Championships. Quite the feat indeed!

The first family we had was the Wilson family. Geoff and Norma Wilson had three talented boys who would all become future champions. That itself was impressive! Graham, who was the eldest boy, came to learn from us. He was first partnered with a beautiful dancer, Debbie Gillard, and they were an incredibly successful partnership. Then Graham partnered Caroline Paidasch, and they were equally successful. Both these partnerships were superb. They all achieved great success, winning many titles and cementing their place in Australia's dancing history. I also have to say Caroline Paidasch was such a beautiful person, both outwardly and in. Her sister Tina was equally wonderful. Here was another beautiful family with successful sisters. Her mother, Violet, always inspired Caroline's grooming and the originality of her competitive dresses. Caroline's outfits, whilst both modern and keeping with the current style at the time, were always elegant. A lovely story to come later!

Graham then danced with Sonia Kruger and they won three Professional Australian Rising Star Championships in all three styles.

Peter Todd and Debbie Todd (source: Shirley Wall).

Graham's two younger twin brothers, Craig and Paul, were both highly successful too. Craig was an Australian Champion and continually made final positions in many Australian Championship events. Craig also made the World Grand final of the Professional 10 Dance in Maastricht, Netherlands with Leeanne Bampton, another successful partnership. They were the only Australian representatives at the event. Paul Wilson teamed up with Donna Reeve, forming one of Australia's greatest and successful partnerships. They were Australian Champions, 3rd in the British Youth Open to the World Standard and second in the Youth Latin.

The second family to come from Wagga Wagga was the Baumer family. Peter and Dawn Baumer gave us three lovely and talented daughters: Debbie, Tanya and Nicole. Debbie, the eldest sister, partnered with Peter Todd and they formed one of the most successful professional partnerships in Australia's dance history. Tanya would go on to win an Australian Championship with Craig Wilson and she was successful with future dance partners too. Nicole was also a very successful dancer with her partner, Stuart Fripp. They would become Junior Champions. Nicole would go on to further success with Neale Byrnes.

The Byrnes brothers, who first learnt with Gwen Wallace, came from Canberra to learn from us. First John and then Neale soon followed. John was an Australian champion with Kim Fraser, a great partnership. He headed to England, where he was quite successful. He was a European 10 Dance champion and 3rd at the British, in the Latin. John now runs a successful studio in England with his wife. They have three children and their daughter is also a dancer.

Neale Brynes had success in Australia, then made his way to the United Kingdom to further his studies and danced with Leslie Thom. They were semifinalists in the British and the World Amateur championships. He then continued on to Canada, where he met his partner (and wife) Nicole. Neale and Nicole have three beautiful daughters and they also run a great studio here in Australia. As a team, they were beautiful dancers and very successful, winning many championship events in Australia. I am so happy to have trained both the boys.

Neale Byrnes and Nicole Byrnes (source: Neale Byrnes).

We also had the Harmer family, whose two daughters Michelle and Stephanie danced. Michelle had great success with Craig Wilson. Stephanie enjoyed her dancing and competed for a short time.

The Taylor family had two beautiful young boys, Aaron and Ryan. Both the Taylor brothers became champion dancers. Ryan had a great career with a lovely girl called Sharon Ware, who was born and lived in the Illawarra Area. The two boys, who, with the support of their family, stayed in the local area with their uncle and aunt to continue their dancing. Aaron would become an Australian and South Pacific junior champion. Aaron, now a successful businessman in the Wollongong area, is organising the wonderful lighting for the National and Australian Championships.

There was the Chang family. They had two sons who were both dancers. Their names were Michael and Justin, and those boys had the utmost respect for their teachers. They were champions, not only pertaining to dancing, but as people too. Mother Colleen and father Simon were incredibly supportive of their sons and would do anything to help them on their dancing journey. Nothing was too much trouble for Simon to do for anyone.

So many families introduced their children into our dance studio. Students who once competed, then after leaving and becoming adults, brought their own children to learn from us. Such families were the Whites and the Iannis. It just shows our longevity and how dancing can still affect someone throughout their life.

As well as learning and competing successfully, everybody had a good time. Local families came and attended our studio and they stayed forever. All great dancing families. So many of them I know and remember (hoping not to forget them by name) but remember each and every one of them, I do. How could I not!

Technique takes over when we lose inspiration.

The Aussie Larrikin

There was always great fun between our dancing couples and some cheekiness, too. Many of them became great friends and some liked to play jokes on each other.

We held our Point Score competition one Sunday afternoon at a community hall in the Northern Suburbs. The boys, who I called *Larrikins,* found an adult magazine in the men's dressing room. Ray was announcing the events over the microphone and concentrating very hard to make sure he was saying the names correctly. Adam, who had not started dancing, was about 6 years old. One of those lovely boys gave the magazine to Adam to give to his father - which he did and Ray's concentration went through the door when he saw it. Adam didn't know, but Ray nearly had a heart attack, as the saying goes. The Larrikins thought it was hilarious to catch Ray out and they laughed their heads off. Ray wasn't impressed, but it was funny. One had to see the surprise look on Ray's face - it was priceless!

When we were at our Woonona studio, five of our outstanding male dancers formed a club by themselves. It was called The Waffle Club. Named after our lovely dessert.

The club members comprised John Byrnes, Mark Sullivan, Ray McMahon, Brett Dorney and Myles West. When we had a free Sunday afternoon, around 3pm, these guys would come out to our house at Thirroul for a visit. I would hear this little choir coming up the back steps chanting, "waffles, waffles." So, every visit I would make them waffles with strawberries and cream.

It was during this time that Peter Todd's mother Rina, (who was affectionately known as Rene) took in three of those boys to look after and house them. Mark, John and Brett became her three extra sons.

Mark Sullivan and Debbie Sullivan (source: Mark Sullivan).

John Byrnes, who was famous for his tomato plants, made up a lovely little song about Rene. It went "Rene, Rene, you dancing machine." Rene was a wonderful lady. She ruled those boys with an iron rod. They respected and loved her very much. Friday night was their dinner night before the practice class. Often, they were joined by other pupils at Rene's house for dinner. Such great times.

These were the years that continued with our success. Everyone was dancing everywhere and really enjoyed themselves. They all looked forward to it. As I mentioned in an earlier chapter, the Federal event ran for three weeks in a row and commencing time was at 6pm, none of this 8.30am business. Imagine having to organise for that start time!

We had a week in between to practice, as not all styles were run in the same week. They weren't short of dancers in the Open Amateur either. After the final six were selected, the next place getters 7 through to 12 were so good that they could have been in the final too!

Most dancing competitions usually ran on a Saturday and our National Championships typically ran over the two days of the weekend. Wherever the championships were held in a particular state, dancers and fans would travel to them. These were the South Pacific, Australasian and the Australian Championships. Everyone organised themselves to stay at a hotel.

Those that could would travel by coach to Melbourne for the Australian Championships. It was a godsend to have had the coach in Melbourne, as they would bus the students back and forth to the hotels and the venue before, during and after the competitions. We stayed in the nicest hotels. I always got a good deal for the tariff, which helped.

We used to have the best parties after the second day of the Championships. Alan and Donna used to travel to the Australian Championships with the studio group via coach. Alan loved it as he would enjoy the wonderful scenery along the way. The presence of both Alan and Donna on board gave all the other pupils a good feeling of being together and one of comradeship. Just like Frank and Peggy Spencer's Penge Team in England.

One Australian, Donna, invited everyone at the competition to come to us after party. She was always so thoughtful. We rented a room, a jukebox and water pistols. It was the greatest party ever! After that year, everyone wanted to come to our party celebrations. Rod Marsh, one of Australia's great cricket players, was also staying at our hotel and he came to the party too!

One of the Waffle gang, Ray McMahon, had a kombi van and each week he would bring down this beautiful fruit cake to us at the studio, courtesy of his firm he worked for. It was so nice for such an ardent dancer. Ray never forgot those who helped him when he needed it, and through his thoughtfulness, donated 12 diamond rings for our South Coast Spectacular, two years in a row! The rings were from his business that he started. The competitors received those prizes with such excitement.

Myles West, another Waffle gang member, was a good mechanic and a talented dancer. He once took Adam's little Honda motor bike back home to Port Kembla for a service. Adam was about 10 at the time, so the bike wasn't very big. Later that week, Myles rode Adam's motorbike back to our house at Thirroul - a good half-hour trip. What made it even more amazing was the fact that Myles is 6 foot tall. Driving that baby bike must have been quite a sight. Myles married and had a lovely family. One of his sons was very talented and became a performer in Cirque du Soleil. A great achievement.

I have to say those boys/ young men had the best times ever. Other Larrikin's - Aaron Taylor, Robert Benge, Howard Whitehall and Simon Christie, then joined them. The enjoyment continued. Not only were those boys outstanding dancers, together they had such a wonderful rapport. We are all still in contact with each other with much love and feeling. They were and still are great people.

Ray McMahon and Sue McMahon (source: Ray McMahon).

Peter and Mark were real Larrikin's and the best of mates. They both got married not long after each other. Mark's wedding reception was such a beautiful day for all of us. Then Peter got married. Peter, the day before his wedding, had quite a lot to drink and nothing to eat. On his wedding day, he had nothing to eat either. Then, as usual with Peter, all the stops were pulled out. Entertainment at its best! Peter fainted, the groomsman fainted, which left the best man, Mark Sullivan, standing alone holding the fort. This little bit of entertainment only contributed to a great day and a gorgeous wedding. Both of my best friends were now married to lovely girls.

Peter Todd and Mark Sullivan were such a great influence. (I say that with tongue in cheek). Once they got married, it did not stop them attending our functions as they danced with their wives, such lovely dancers, Debbie Todd and Debbie Sullivan. Everyday Peter Todd and I have a laugh about the past. He calls me on the phone to check in on me and it just makes my day with the memories and visits me every Thursday for coffee. I really enjoy this time.

One more couple who tied the knot were Jacob Hall and Rachelle Grant. They were lovely people and beautiful, successful dancers. Rachelle came from New Zealand and Jacob was from Thirroul. Their wedding was one of the most beautiful weddings I have ever been to. Both of them had lovely, supportive families. Jacob was one of my last talented juniors that I taught from the beginning.

Great dancers are not great because of their technique.

They are great because of their passion.

Hong Kong and Taiwan

My dancing has taken me around the world. Paul Bishop was a British Senior Professional Champion who taught ballroom dancing in Hong Kong at his dance academy. It was through him I was invited to adjudicate, lecture and teach on two occasions. I absolutely loved Hong Kong. It was such an exciting place.

My first trip was in 1987 and on the second trip, we also went to Macau and visited the gambling casino. I had never seen anything like it. They showed us the utmost respect and hospitality. The 1987 trip was for an International Competition. Competitors were invited from Australia, Europe and Hong Kong, comprising two Junior and several Adult couples. Everything was, "Mickey Mouse" as the saying goes.

This particular event had already been running for two years. The 1987 event was used to promote and introduce Ballroom Dancing into mainland China. The event was sponsored with a generous donation by Mr. Stanely Ho, a well-known casino mogul and businessman. He was also a patron of the Hong Kong Ballet Group and an avid ballroom dancer who really had a love for the arts.

One supporter of the Australian team was Mr. Keith Whatman. Keith was the owner of the Broadway Ballroom at 173 Broadway Street, where the original building stood. It was called the Broadway Theatre and built in 1911. Over the years, it changed hands and became a venue for live bands. In 1972, there was a major fire that completely destroyed the interior. It sat in this condition for four years, yet the outside of the building was intact. Keith purchased the venue and began its refurbishment and converting the fire ravaged theatre into one big ballroom. At the Broadway Ballroom, they held dance classes and competitions. The Broadway Ballroom ran only for four years, yet Keith continued to support ballroom dancing after it closed. We affectionately knew Keith as *'Whatman the Wrecker'*, as his day job was in demolition. He was well-known for the buildings that he demolished all over Sydney.

One particular year that our studio was going to the Australian Championships, a large group of our students flew to Melbourne. Mr. Whatman came with us as well. During the journey, whilst in the air, the airline companies went on strike. As a result, they would not let us get our luggage off the plane when we landed. We needed our clothes to access all the competition attire. So, with some know-how and persuasion, Ray and Mr. Whatman, after much explanation that the girls would need to dance in their events, pleaded with the airline staff to retrieve their costumes, which had been impounded. The airline gave in and gave permission for Ray and Keith to take delivery of their luggage. Keith then took all our students to dinner because they were upset. We always tried to stay at the Melbourne Sofitel Hotel. They were and still are good for the dancers. We looked after Keith and he always wanted to be included.

Keith attended the Hong Kong event, where the Junior Competition was controversially won by an English couple. They weren't one of their best couples. The second night of the competition was by popular vote for the Juniors, so our adult couples thought they would help out. The young men opted to put themselves in each corner of the ballroom. They knew exactly what they were doing. When they calculated the applause from the stirring of the crowd by our corner cheerleaders, our junior couple won, who, incidentally, were Adam Reeve and Samantha Hutchison. They won by a mile. They received for their prize, a RAND, which is a South African Gold coin. The four corner cheerleaders were Neale Byrnes, Michael Withers, Glen Akhurst and Chris Milburn.

Mr. Whatman then took us to a nightclub. I was concerned about our junior couple going, but they said everything was alright. The nightclub turned out to be the famous Volvo Hostess Club. The hostesses formed a guard of honour when we entered the club, much to Adam's concern as they giggled and pinched him on the cheek.

Our group danced for the guests to a magnificent band and the organisers also got Adam to do some rap dancing. Then a most unusual thing happened. When the men needed to get to the bathroom, which was lavish, a Rolls Royce vehicle (full sized) picked them up and drove them there. That's how big the club was! By the way, the ladies' bathroom was very basic and one had to walk.

When one of the male clients of the club wanted to light a cigarette, a hostess would rush over and light it for him. The clients also received a bottle of Johnny Walker Black Label Scotch. They wanted our team to come back the next night, on one condition: that Adam should dance his rap routine again. I didn't think that Adam should dance that late, between 12 and 1 o'clock in the morning. I phoned Ray and checked with him and he thought that this one time would be OK.

All the dancers were reimbursed very well towards their trips. The money was great! Funnily enough, each night we went to the club, we told none of the other dancers. One German guy was very curious and he would always ask us where we were going. We just replied that we were going out for dinner.

In 1989, we went to Taiwan. The trip was great. Mr. Tang, the chairman of the Pan German Universal Motors Group, invited our team from the studio. Whilst on a trip to Australia, he visited our studio for lessons and he loved our couples, hence the invitation to his show. It was part of their huge promotion of the latest and luxury cars from all over the world. Around 30,000 people attended the show each day.

They laid out a beautiful new floor for our students to perform on. The building was enormous. I was the host and spoke a little

Chinese, such as greetings and introducing the show. Ray, on the other hand, used an interpreter - he used his brains.

I tried to use a little bit of circus and the crowd loved it. Our team was composed of an Amateur couple, Paul Wilson and Donna Reeve; the Youth couple, Adam Reeve and Samantha Hutchison; the Junior couple, Jacob James and Lisa Atkinson and the Juvenile couple, Grant Barratt-Thompson and Christie Atkinson. After they danced, our host gave them a lovely time. I also fitted in lectures and lessons for the Taiwanese competitive dancers. There were some lovely dancers amongst them.

It was Christmas time and Mr. Tang gave all the dancers in our team presents even though they didn't celebrate Christmas in Taiwan. As well as paying return air fares and accommodation, Mr. Tang also paid for two mothers to come along on our trip as chaperones.

We really saw a lot of Taipei. Mr. Tang loved our dancers so much; he booked us again a couple of years later. Same commitment, but not at Christmas. We had a great rapport with him. It was sad when he passed.

I loved Taiwan and Hong Kong. Everything we wanted was available to us. Our host arranged for all that we needed. Mr. Tang was so thoughtful. His associates that worked for him were our bodyguards. We were taken everywhere and wanted for nothing. At one point, we thought we had left one boy behind. We were extremely lucky as one bodyguard had him with him - much relief.

Competitive alertness for strategy.

Tributes

I have met so many appreciative people in my life through dancing from all walks of life. Whether they were humble spectators, one of my peers, fellow teachers or colleagues, any praise they were kind enough to give me was always received with appreciation with heartfelt gratitude. I love what I do; I love the dance and it is humbling when written acknowledgements and tributes come via the way of letters, emails or in print. The following are just a few of the lovely tributes that both Ray and I have received over the years and I just want to take this moment to say thank you to those who took the time to write these lovely words and gestures of kindness.

Louise Turk wrote the following passage for the Illawarra Mercury on August 6, 2011. It was featured in the Weekender section on page 6:

'Having a ball'

Together with her husband and dance partner Ray, Margaret Reeve ruled the dance world for years. Both are still heavily involved in the sport, writes LOUISE TURK.

It's been 40 years since MARGARET Reeve officially retired from the world of ballroom dancing, ending a 10 - year reign, which she shared with husband Ray, as undefeated Australian Professional Champions.

Today, Margaret, 72, still retains an air of glamour and a certain poise that makes her easy to spot as she walks down Wollongong's Crown Street Mall, dressed head-to-toe in chic black with her hair pulled back tightly off her face ballerina-style. She still has the thin, elegant fingers, which added to her alluring beauty on the dance floor, when they were placed prominently on her husband's left shoulder.

In the 1960s, Thirrouls' Ray and Margaret - known professionally as Reeve and Maloney - represented Australia in national and international competitions, winning many titles and developing a high profile.

Margaret may have left behind her position in the spotlight in 1971, but she remains as connected as ever to the world of ballroom dancing. This week the energetic woman with a hearty laugh is putting the final touches on an event which bears her stamp - the annual South Coast Ballroom Dancesport Spectacular.

Ray, 80, and Margaret have been organising the glittering event, which attracts competitors from across Australia and some international dancers, for the past 48 years.

"I really enjoy meeting the young, talented people of our region. It keeps me active and young," Margaret says of her involvement with the spectacular. "I love the rhythm and expression of dance. I love music, any type of music. It's wonderful to see people dancing around to lovely music and to watch their self-expression."

It's a strong statement of the Reeves' love of ballroom dancing that they continue to drive the competition, after retiring in 2006 from running their long-established Reeve Dance Academy.

The Reeves' children, Donna and Adam, and their respective partners, Alan Shingler and Karen Reeve, took over the reins and re-established the business as Dancespace 383. In a nice piece of symmetry, Dancespace 383's Crown St, Wollongong, studio was the venue for the Reeves` inaugural dancesport spectacular in 1953.

The 2011 event to be held in the newly refurbished Wollongong Town Hall on August 14 is no easy task to organise. There will be 27 international judges to adjudicate the three different styles: Modern, Latin American and New Vogue. More than 100 amateur couples in junior and senior age categories will compete. The field will include social dancers and beginners as well as those who dance regularly on the competition circuit. In addition to cash prizes and trophies for winners, sample bags are handed out to the tiny tot participants.

Ray, dressed in a sharp dinner suit, and Margaret, kitted out in dazzling evening wear, will be Ballroom's grand couple of the day, but they are unlikely to dance. "We'll be too busy for that," Margaret laughs.

The Reeve partnership began in 1958 when 17-year-old Margaret Maloney turned up for dance lessons with Ray, who was then teaching at the Thirroul RSL Hall. "I always wanted to dance," she says.

"I grew up in Leichhardt and went to school with kids who would go on to become some of the biggest names in dancing - the Honeybrooks, the Breens and the Roberts."

Ray, a cabinetmaker by trade, started teaching dance in his spare time in 1953. Ray's mother used to ring up his employer and say: "Ray won't be in today; he's had a hard night - dancing." Margaret chuckles.

Ray and Margaret's relationship soon moved from teacher and student to dancing partners on stage and partners in life. They married in 1961. Margaret changed her name to Reeve but was still known on the competition circuit by her maiden name.

Ray and Margaret, who were technically brilliant and possessed great stamina and perfect coordination, began to enjoy enormous success as dance partners. "We were grand finalists at world championships and we were the triple undefeated Australasian and South Pacific professional champions," Margaret says. "I think our continuity of movement was our big thing."

Margaret says their success was also due to a good dose of hard work and determination. "We practiced every day of our lives," she recalls. "We'd practice from 10am to midday and our coach used to tell us to have a lie down in the afternoon. Then we'd teach from 5pm to 10pm every night and that was hard work physically. On the weekends, we did floor shows."

Their triumphs on the dance floor led to a boom in students at the Reeve Academy of Dance, which operated at Thirroul for 25 years and then from a Princes Hwy studio at Woonona for another 30 years. Together, Ray and Margaret trained multiple Australian champion dancers and numerous *international champions. Their studio was considered one of Australia's main breeding grounds for future champions.*

"I wouldn't change anything about my life - good or bad," Margaret says. "It's been a great journey. We've seen wonderful dancers and places. We've been very, very proud of our children's accomplishments."

The Reeve's children took up dancing from a young age and went on to marry their dance partners. "We did everything together as a family. They were fabulous years," reflects Margaret.

Donna and her UK-born husband and dance partner Alan Shingler were the 1998 British Standard Ballroom Champions. The former Thirroul girl won every major title in Australia from an eight-year-old juvenile up to the Australian professional circuit before a stellar international career with Alan.

At the pinnacle of Adam's ballroom dancing career, he and his Icelandic wife Karen out-danced couples from 30 countries to be named World Professional 10 Dance Champions 2003. Both were original cast members of the world-famous stage show Burn the Floor.

The four dancers - all of whom are directors at Dancespace 383 - are among the most highly recognised dancesport couples in the world.

As well as organising the annual spectacular, Margaret also lends her professional skills and expertise to dancers who are studying to become adjudicators. Margaret still dances occasionally but adds: "I don't run around the floor at 50 miles an hour anymore."

She no longer dances with Ray, but the pair who would be celebrating 50 years of marriage, remain close. They are devoted to their four grandchildren: Freyja, Charley, Briet and Soley.

Dancespace 383 is a hive of activity early in the morning when Margaret is organising the promotion of the dancesport spectacular. There is a middle-aged couple from Perth practicing their moves with Donna and a group of young dancers chatting near the studio wall, which is lined with trophies.

Louise Turk - Illawarra Mercury.

A fabulous family:
`The dancing Reeve`s churn out the champs`

I have often expressed my astonishment at the ceaseless parade of world class talent that has emerged from the Illawarra Region, especially in the arts. There seems to be no stopping the avalanche of stars making their mark on the world stage.

You all know the people, I mean. Those like Anthony Warlow, Richard Tognetti and Amber Lyn Hammond. Some of our superstars don't command the same glare of publicity, but their global achievements are just spectacular. As a judge on the St George Youth Endeavour Award panel, I come across artistic brilliance all the time. This week an award went to a young man named Adam Reeve who is a world class ballroom dancer. When the awards were handed out this week, Adam wasn't there because he was representing his country at a championship event in Miami. Adam's mother Margaret was there to collect her son's award. Beside her was her husband, Ray.

We chatted about Adam's incredible accomplishments. Then we chatted about their daughter Donna and her great achievements. This was a good story, a fine column, I thought. We made arrangements to meet at Ray and Margaret's ballroom dancing studio in Woonona to continue our talks.

When I walked in, I was confronted by a long table covered with press clippings, photographs and exhaustive and voluminous accounts of the feats of the Reeve family. To my eternal shame, I had to confess my ignorance of the remarkable feats of Ray and Margaret Reeve. I knew they were good, very good. Heavens above. They too were almost world champions.

For ten years in this country, they were unconquerable, reigning champions in ballroom dancing, superstars who carried off trophies and blazed in the glare of entertainment headlines. There they were splashed across the front page of the Illawarra Mercury, the Daily Telegraph, women's magazines and national journals. And now their son, Adam, and daughter, Donna, were dazzling judges all over the world.

You look around the studio and see trophies, hundreds of them. You don't know where to start. They are symbols of the dominance and stunning brilliance of this family. How often in life do you find mother, father, daughter and son strutting the world stage, beaten the best in the universe and unbeatable in their own country?

The Reeves do more than that. They churn out ballroom dancing champions as though there's no tomorrow. Dozens and dozens of them. People come from all over the world to learn from them.

Two Swiss teenagers turned up one day at Woonona, backpacks and bicycles, to find the studio. A rich American and his wife came out on the QE2 just to learn ballroom dancing from them. The Reeve's family has been fated and acclaimed the world over.

But this week, when Ray and Margaret were present for Adam's award, they were so proud they almost wept. You know why? Adam was recognised and honored by his own city. That means more to them than anything. A lovely family. They rate as one of the remarkable achievements of the Illawarra.

Peter Cullen - Illawarra Mercury

The Maker of Champions
By Glen Tierny

Having returned from the ADS Australian, I am moved to write the following about Ray Reeve.

A great coach can communicate the simple things that are then developed into advanced principles which produce quality movement, shape and performance, underpinned by sound technique.

A couple trained by a great coach develops a knowledge and self-belief that leads them to search for their own individual style and quality with strong self-motivation.

Ray Reeve has produced champions year after year over my entire lifetime and although I am motivated by my recognition, my life is enriched by the success my couples enjoy. I can't begin to appreciate the pride that he and Margaret must have felt in Melbourne to see their children, Donna and Adam with their partners, now two of the World's best professional couples.

I consider any opportunity to sit and talk to Ray Reeve as a valuable lesson and when he suggests to me that he may soon consider, "hanging up his judging shoes" I am sad indeed.

I don't ever recall reading about Ray Reeve as Australia's greatest ever Ballroom coach. It seems to me that it is past time that these words were written and I offer my congratulations to Ray and Margaret together with Donna and Alan, Adam and Karen, on what could be considered a culmination of a lifetime's work and dedication.

The following tributes are all in relation to our studio, celebrating 50 years of operation. Donna and Adam, along with their spouses Alan and Karen, planned a most magnificent event of world class, held here in the Wollongong region. The Oz Dance Camp. It also was the perfect draw card for our 50th anniversary.

A tribute to Ray & Margaret Reeve

Ray and Margaret are celebrating 50 years of dancing on the South Coast. The Reeve Dance Studio opened in late 1953. Ray, a local boy, teamed up with Margaret, a Sydney girl, and started a partnership that was to become world famous -through themselves and their children.

They first had a successful competitive career in Australia, winning all the major events and then going on to achieve world status by becoming World Standard Professional Grand Finalists.

A few years later, they teamed up to have their first-born child "Donna" and a few years later, their son "Adam". Both have continued the family's competitive success.

But it has been as teachers that they have excelled and have made an indelible mark on Australia's dancing history. Their very first student Kerry Wilson - who walked into the studio in Thirroul at age 10 and went on to become a World Professional Finalist. From there, the list goes on. Every name you can mention on the Australian dancing scene today has walked through their studio, many of which have gone on to international success. They were part of the Golden Era of Australian Dancing, where Australian couples had major success on the international circuit. Their coaching and insight helped many Australians achieve the much dreamed about `International Success`.

What is the true inspiration of Ray and Margaret is that even at their age, they still have an undying passion for dance. It is that passion that has brought them the success and respect that they have drawn over the last 50 years. Two great pioneers of Australian Dancing - we give our thanks.

Article in the Valentine Ball Program of the first Oz Dance Camp.

This was an email dated January 1st, 2004

Dear Ray and Margaret,

It is already forty years ago when you, and Toshi and I, together with Bill/Bobbie Irvine, Eggleton, enjoyed a dance travel. Toshi passed away nine years ago. 1965 was an unforgettable, wonderful year for me. In that year, we came to be acquainted with you through the introduction of Mr. Alex Moore and we started our pleasant dance journey, didn't we?

Two years ago, Donna came to see me when she visited Japan. It was a wonderful surprise to know for the first time that Donna was your dear daughter. I remember her well, as I have seen her dancing beautifully several times in Blackpool, whose wonderful dance impressed me deeply.

I have not seen Adam yet, but I am glad to tell you that the couple has grown into first-class excellent dancers. My son Masatoshi-Mari is now active as a B-class competitor. There are 4 classes A, B, C, D starting from D, being judged by the results of this dance world. He is now working hard aiming at becoming a champion in the future.

Now I would like to offer my hearty congratulations upon the 50th anniversary of the foundation of your studio. On the occasion of the party for celebrating the 50th anniversary, I hear that the lectures will be given by John Wood and Richard Porter and that three demonstrations will be shown.

I wish you, from the bottom of my heart, continued prosperity and success.

Yours sincerely,

Makato Seki

Email dated December 15, 2003

Dear Ray and Margaret, Karen and I would like to wish you both sincere congratulations on the special 50th anniversary of your dance business! It is a marvelous achievement and one that is; we are sure, backed by the whole dance profession, not only in Australia but all over the world.

We have known you both as acquaintances over many years and are aware of the many dancers and champions that have passed through your dance school doors. We know you must be very proud of both your siblings, Adam, with Karen who achieved the very high distinction World's Professional 10 Dance Champions, earlier this year and of course your gorgeous daughter Donna with Alan who seemed to go from strength to strength this year in their performance and who danced the most beautiful waltz at this year's Night of 1000 Stars, in London, one of the special moments in my life.

Both Karen, Henry and I would like to wish you continued success in your future and here's to the next 50 years in this wonderful business that we call ballroom dancing. Our love to you both for a wonderful Christmas and a Happy and Healthy New Year!!

Our love, Marcus, Karen and Henry James Hilton xx xx xx

M Hilton MBE.

Email dated February 3rd, 2004

Dear Margaret and Ray,

Congratulations.

It gives me a great deal of pleasure to be sending these very special wishes to you. 50 years. I can't believe it. Even though I have lived in England for the past 30 years, I have some wonderful memories of the years I spent travelling to Thirroul for lessons. Monday evenings were a busy time. With Latin lessons with Marg, Ballroom with Ray and New Vogue with John Minogue. Where did we find the energy? Through all your hard work and dedication to our wonderful business, you have helped in many ways to develop, not only Australian Champions in all three styles, but World and British Ballroom Champions. And of course, let's not forget your two very talented children who we have had the good fortune of carrying on your good work with. What more can one say but THANK YOU for the part you played in my future? My Aussie roots show from time to time, I often say you are both bloody good teachers!!!!!!!!!!! Keep up the good work all my love and best wishes for this happy occasion and sorry I can't be with you love Marion.

Marion Welsh.

Emailed dated February 3rd, 2004

Dear Ray and Margaret,

Many many congratulations on your 50th anniversary of your studio and your teaching in Australia.

It was about this time 31 years ago that Marion and I left Sydney to go to London for a very exciting time. The attached photo of Marion and myself leaving Sydney with Margaret, Donna and Adam there to wave goodbye meant a great deal to us.

The success we achieved in Australia and later internationally came a lot from the lessons, training and friendship received in Australia from both of you.

Australian dancing owes you both a great debt, not only for the style and quality of your own dancing, but the way you tirelessly worked with your many couples to mould, cajole, inspire and teach so many Australian Champions, International Champions and World Champions.

I am sure that of all the dancers you worked with, the fantastic achievements of Donna and Adam give you much pleasure. Each time I see them dancing at major championships, I invariably think of you both.

Ray and Margaret, thank you once again for the lessons, and support you gave us, the great meals and parties we used to have at your house.

Have a great celebration. You deserve it.

Greg and Jeanny Smith.

Another tribute from England

Dear Ray and Margaret,

We would both like to send you many, many congratulations on reaching the 50th anniversary of your dance school.

You must be so proud to have reached this fantastic achievement, spanning through so many generations of dance, and being able to cherish many memories.

You truly have had a lifetime of dance, firstly securing an exciting competitive career yourselves, and then famously producing many of Australia's finest dancers, which we are sure you will continue to do in the future. Of course, two of the most famous and widely successful dancers to have been born out of your studio are your very own children, Donna and Adam.

You must be so proud and elated at their achievements knowing that, (together with Alan and Karen), their knowledge and performances, thrill, excite and educate audiences throughout the World.

We hope that today will be a fantastic memory of the last 50 years, and that you will be able to relax and enjoy spending time with your family and friends from both home and abroad.

Congratulations once again and here is to the next fifty years with our very best wishes, Timothy and Joanne.

Timothy Howson and Joanne Bolton.

PRIME MINISTER
CANBERRA

MESSAGE: RAY AND MARGARET REEVE – 50TH ANNIVERSARY AS PRINCIPALS OF THE REEVE ACADEMY OF DANCING

I am delighted to have the opportunity to provide this message to mark the 50th anniversary of Ray and Margaret Reeve as principals of the Reeve Academy of Dancing.

Ballroom dancing is a vibrant and exciting sport that has a large and devoted following in Australia. It is unique in its incorporation of a range of cross cultural influences and the active participation of all age groups.

Ray and Margaret Reeve have devoted more than fifty years to Australian dancing, first as dancers, then as teachers. This is a significant achievement. Their dedication to supporting Australian dancing has been outstanding and the Reeve Academy of Dancing continues to set the highest standard of excellence. Both their children are also internationally acclaimed dancers and are committed to promoting the industry through such events as the Oz Dance Camp, which is being held for the first time in Australia.

I am sure all those present this evening and all those who have been associated with the Reeve Academy of Dancing, will join with me in wishing Ray and Margaret all the best for the future.

(John Howard)

It really is such a blessing to be acknowledged by so many in so many ways. Even though the achievements have been high, it is the moments and memories that truly count. Something as simple as a grandparent who came to see their grandchild dance in a show and then come up and say, "What a wonderful day it was." When you see their joy, that is the ultimate recognition.

The most wonderful surprise we received was at our 50th Anniversary Party, Valentine Ball. It was a letter from the then Australian Prime Minister, The Honourable John Howard. It truly was a magical night and a memory we shall cherish.

We used persistence and tenacity

To develop our ideas in our teaching

Where we got our information from

We live in the age of information. With information everywhere, there really is no excuse for not knowing. So where did we get our information from? All the different dancing societies had secretaries and committees who achieved their goal of getting information out to the dance studios. They let them know about the running of events, dates, times and how to purchase tickets.

When I first started dancing and competing, all the information about dancing events came from Ray at the studio. He would be informed about what was coming up and relayed the information to all the dance students. Ray would get information from Eileen Kane and others. Going to a competition itself was a great way that networking would happen. Someone would come up and introduce themselves. They informed you they were holding an event or competition and this was another way that our students knew about what was making the rounds. It may have been a competition run by another society or even a private promoter. We always had pamphlets and flyers all over the studio as constant reminders of events. The state of NSW had such a powerful hold when it came to competitions. There was always a competition going on somewhere on the weekend. One certainly had the option to pick and choose what competition to go to and for some of the top competitors, this became important, because it could easily become too much competition every weekend. A balance had to be found.

Not every competition was a championship event, but every competition was a chance to craft your talent. It gave couples so much opportunity to practice competition and to see what the world of competitive ballroom dancing was really like. Oh, and the number of competitors was staggering! There were so many competitors that it warranted having a competition every weekend. It seemed like everyone was dancing.

Competition entry was completely up to the individual. The studios would register couples and would send their nominations to the society running the event. This was the way they could really run their shows and events, by knowing the number of competitors from the outset. It eased the flow by keeping the circle moving from society to studio to competitor.

In 1931, the Federal Association of Teachers of Dancing (F.A.T.D) was formed in Australia for dancing teachers of all styles. In the 1940s, they separated the Theatrical division from the Ballroom Dancing division, as there was a great need because of its rapid growth. In 1947, Eileen Kane was appointed as the full-time secretary. Eileen held this position for almost forty years.

Eileen Kane was brilliant at letting people know about the F.A.T.D events. As I was the vice president, we were the only society to have a full-time secretary with a full-time office that operated five days a week. At that time, one could purchase books and papers pertaining to information about the dancing profession and become informed of dancing events. Federal was affiliated with the I.S.T.D society - an English society that in the early days gave out a lot of information both in ballet and other styles. Eileen, in her tenacity, ran the office with decorum and efficiency. When it came to the competitions, no one except the examiners and judges were allowed on the stage whilst the competitions were in progress. She ran a tight ship.

I know that we have good communication with today's technology, but there was no one like her! For upcoming events by Federal, Eileen would send out a circular to every studio and professional teacher, giving the information required. It wasn't just sending out circulars, but every day Eileen was on the phone with members of the society and other dancers. I still think that the personal connection, whether by phone, post or internet and social media is the best way to let people know what's going on.

Every form of information must be covered. For me, the telephone is great. As I mentioned earlier, we had no Latin American theory books. Prior to that, we had to rely on the senior teachers of the day to write the theory down in notes during a lesson, to learn the basic technique for our exams. Then a Latin Technique book was printed around 1965.

In England, at the time, you could go to the local newspaper stand and purchase a copy of the Dancing Times. The Dancing Times gave out great information. A young couple, Colin and Joy Hillary, started a monthly publication called the Australian Dancing Times, and this added to our information. After a few years, they moved to Miami, USA.

In 1989, after some years with no publication, the national Australian Dance Review (ADR) started. In fact, the ADR was well received internationally. The ADR was run under the direction of Barry and Shirley Wall, while they also ran their own studio. Barry and Shirley, with their expertise, worked so hard to give us all the information on the local, national and international results of our dancers. It kept us busy each month to look to see who was in the latest edition. They continued on successfully for a long time and the magazine just kept getting better with a lovely photo on the front cover of champions and eventually the magazine was presented in colour.

Every month, the information was excellent, including competition results, photos and write-ups. All over Australia, dancers hurried to purchase a copy of the Review to see who was on the cover and to see if their results were in it. Wonderful articles were written, carrying on from other journals, which gave us a world of knowledge. The studios would sell editions of the ADR and I assure you they were all gone the week we put them on our studio desk.

One of the nicest things I had ever seen written was when Barry commented about Donna. THE DROUGHT HAS BROKEN! It was in relation to Donna and Alan winning the British Championships. This meant so much to me. It had been years since an Australian had won the British Open.

Barry and Shirley Wall had two lovely girls, Melinda and Kylie. They, too, were successful. Melinda danced with Adam and they had a successful career, culminating with them making the Grand Final of the Amateur World 10 Dance Championships in Verona, Italy. Kylie would go on to open her own studio.

Once I started competing with Ray, we were in contact with overseas studios and teachers. It was a way of putting our names out there. Then, after our trip to England in 1965, our names were recognised. We developed more connections and even formed many friendships. Over the years, this made it easier for us when travelling, teaching or judging. We had carved out a name for ourselves by constant communication and keeping connected. We worked really hard at promoting our studio and our dancers. It wasn't about looking at us; it was about running our business. For so many years, all we had to rely upon was the telephone or the mail for our information. Staying in touch with people and on top of what was happening at the time was paramount to running our studio. Even though we had social dancing and medal tests at our studio, competitions were really the life line for running our dance academy.

One advantage of not having social media back in the day was that everyone would expect phone calls, letters or flyers to come through, so they were always answered. Otherwise, the dancing would never have functioned. If I had to guess how many phone calls and meetings with people, I have had over the years in relation to keeping our students informed, I wouldn't know where to begin.

Every time you step onto the dance floor,

you have an opportunity to improve

and grow as a dancer.

Embrace the challenge and have fun.

Students and teaching

Dance came to me in a strange way. As I was watching and listening from the small ballet school near our home in Sydney, little did I know that someday that was going to be me, only in a different style of dance.

When I first taught, I found it very nerve-racking. I really wanted to teach, but I was so nervous. I even said to one young man in class, "Hello, how are you tonight? It's freezing hot, isn't it?" As I taught more and more, the nervousness faded away. The people that I taught were of all ages. They really wanted to dance. Everyone from the individual student to the children who came to our Saturday morning classes.

Many champions came out of that Saturday morning class. It was up and running in the Raymond Road studio when I came into it and it grew in such a delightful way.

We had many children to choose from, but the talented ones came to the top of the class and continued the talent of their expertise.

The format for the classes we kept the same for years and years, because we felt it worked well and produced results. Our students ranged from 5 to 16 years. The Saturday morning children's class ran for 1 hour. The order would be Modern first, New Vogue second and Latin third, finishing with our progressive dances in a circle.

It comprised Waltz, Quickstep, Slow Rhythm, some New Vogue dances, Cha Cha Cha, Samba and Jive. Each style section would run for about 15 minutes. We would typically have boys in a one line, girls facing them in another line. We then walked and danced through the steps, partnering each other before moving onto the next section. We finished with the progressive circle for the last 15 minutes of the class.

Douglas Newton and Candy Lane.

Straight after the morning class was finished, we then ran a Medal class for those students wishing to go for their medal test. It was a chance for students to improve their dancing, learn new choreography and to go to the next level - if they so desired.

Medal tests at the time comprised: Elementary Modern, with the dances being Waltz, Slow Rhythm and Quickstep. Elementary Latin, with the dances being Rumba, Samba and Jive. Bronze Modern Medals were Waltz, Foxtrot, Slow Rhythm and Quickstep. Bronze Latin was Rumba, Samba, Paso Doble and Jive. Cha Cha, was usually a Medal on its own. For the Silver Modern, the addition of the Quick Rhythm and Tango was added for the Junior's and up.

Kerry Wilson - one of our greatest dancers, was the first lesson that I ever gave and, as I mentioned in a previous chapter, my very first student. After showing Kerry the fundamentals, I danced with him. When Kerry attended the Thursday night class, along with his parents. He would dance with all the advanced girls. At such an early age, he had worked it out: the more one danced with advanced dancers, the more one would improve. He then decided to have a weekly lesson with me. His achievements were outstanding.

After Kerry Wilson, my student numbers grew. I then taught my younger people and put some together as couples. With much passion in my teaching and a great intensity to go forward, my teaching developed.

It was so good to put a new couple together and watch their development. I was good at motivating couples competing in the championships. There were many things that contributed to preparation. To develop and prepare, nearly all couples in a lesson learn how to achieve and improve their movement.

Our Beginner students all had different ways of learning. Ray and I would show them their foot positions and then we would dance with them. We, too, could feel their interpretation as they progressed. Given a good foundation with their technique, we then danced with each pupil to give them a feeling from both Ray and I, to nurture their feelings that we felt through the use of their bodies. Once again, foot rhythm and body rhythm, always with a lovely feel, enhancing the picture made by their dancing.

John Byrnes and Kim Fraser (source: Kim Dorney).

The students improved each week. They tried so hard and it all paid off. Sometimes they became frustrated, but I, knowing that they were talented, would motivate them in any way I could to quash their doubts.

Motivation comes in all shapes and sizes and I tried so hard to accommodate all our pupils. From Beginner to Amateur. The A grade took on so much and they needed to motivate themselves with their teachers' help. Anyone can learn the technique; the point is to understand it. Using the power of learning, feeling and motivation together can form the recipe to start one's journey. The pupils that really wanted to dance took on everything that was thrown at them. Their results came faster, which in any sport, those who want to do something really well will float to the top and become successful.

I gave my students' confidence, but it was difficult to take them to the next level. If our pupils were ever down in spirit, I would always uplift them by sending them on their way with a more positive approach. I gave a lot of single lessons that erupted, creating such wonderful dancers. Many would go on to become champions.

It was our teaching and demonstrating that captured the hearts of students everywhere. It was such a buzz at the time, everything was happening - teaching, England and competing in the World and British Championships. Our teaching took us all around Australia. We travelled to dance studios in every state to teach their top couples - bar none. Other teachers, in turn, would encourage their own couples to visit us and travel to our studio. This happened many times in both of our locations. One such time was at our Thirroul studio. Ray had recently traveled to Perth to do some teaching. Derek Gatley, who ran a WRIGHTSON`S franchise studio in Perth, liked Ray's teaching so much, he took it upon himself to organise a week of lessons at our studio with several of his top couples. He organised cheap accommodation at local hotels in the area. For one crazy week, we had back-to-back lessons with his couples, as well as teaching our own couples with a full studio roster. It was really great.

Stefano Olivieri and Karina Schembri.

We looked after all the grades at our studio, grading pupils according to their ability. Beginners, who often rose to a national and international standard, would further their learning abroad. Many of our students opened their own studios throughout Australia. Some of them moved to other countries to live and to teach - England,

Iceland, Denmark, Netherlands, New Zealand, Hong Kong, USA and Canada. They were frequented by many other pupils as well.

Many overseas professionals came to our studio and we never stopped expanding our knowledge. It grew with a passion. There were tours of New Zealand, many times, teaching and demonstrations and all the lovely people we encountered.

I also taught in all the local schools - St Mary's Star of the Sea College, Edmund Rice College, Holy Spirit, St Columbkille`s, St Therese Catholic School, Tigs, Thirroul Primary, St Michaels, Coledale Primary, Woonona High School and Bulli High School. You name it; we went there!

They would have their end-of-year dances and we were so busy that we would have to take some of our other teachers with us to help out. The studio still does this, though it differs greatly from today's end-of-year dances. When we taught the school students, they danced together properly, gaining their know-how from the classes.

Australia has produced some fine Latin American dancers. Not one couple looked the same. Every competing country had their own champions. Some of our champions were internationally successful. They all had their own persona and way of expressing their style and rhythm of each dance. They all had their own dignified performance, which I enjoyed.

Very few dancers affected me emotionally, except for the ones I will mention here. These couples learnt their technique well and applied their own self musicality. They were - Robert and Helen Richey, **Tony Gauci and Dianne Wills-Johnson,** Jason Gilkison and Peta Roby, Barry and Cheryl Wrightson, Paul Green and Karen Rufus, Philip and Jan Nicholas, Larry and Kerry Clarke, Stephen and Carrine Octigan, Neale and Nicole Byrnes.

Our 10 dance Modern and Latin Couples - Greg Smith and Marion Alleyne, Paul Wilson and Donna Reeve, Adam and Karen

Reeve, Douglas Newton and Rosalyn Toulmin, Douglas Newton and Candy Lane, Greg Smith and Rosalyn Smith, Clive Phillips and Karen Phillips, John Byrnes and Kim Fraser, Philip Logan and Norma Lee, Mark and Debbie Sullivan, Alex and Julie Schembri, Stefano Olivieri and Antonella Zucco, Stefano Oliveri and Karina Schembri, Peter and Debbie Todd, Robert McKay and Virginia Chesher. All of these couples were very successful. Dancing won and created a great time for everyone.

My most joyous moments were teaching my children and then the top couples all over Australia. I was so thrilled to teach them all. I once asked some of my students why they started dancing.

Alan Shingler - started dancing to get out of going shopping with his mother on a Saturday morning and of course got a packet of chips and a can of drink. He became a British Champion.

Mark Sullivan - was already dancing, but I had to tell his story. Mark was dancing in New Zealand and he and his new partner were the only couple on the team representing NSW who were not from our studio. Upon returning home to Newcastle from his New Zealand trip, he told his grandmother that he wanted to come down to us to further his learning. His statement was, "they must be doing something right down there. I was the only couple not trained by them" - meaning us. So, Mark came down from Newcastle each Friday night, by train, to have his lessons and he would stay with us. He slept on a blow-up bed on our lounge room floor and would then return home to Newcastle on Sunday night by train. When he moved down to the South Coast, he stayed at Rene Todd's - Peter's mother's was a famous house for the dancers. They were very well looked after.

Peter Todd - why did you start to dance? "I had to go with my sister to accompany her on the bus to the studio, so I thought I would try it and I liked it. Hence, at my age, I am still heavily involved with dancing." Peter married Debbie Baumer and continued with a successful career. He ended up South Pacific, Australasian and

Australian Champion. Peter and Debbie specialised in the New Vogue style, but also won Modern and Latin Championships. Later, Peter became a very successful teacher and produced many champions.

After a very successful amateur career with Karina Schembri, Stefano Olivieri teamed up with Melanie Sears, from Adelaide and their big success was the Professional W.D.S.F. World New Vogue Championships in Melbourne. Peter trained Stefano and Melanie to win this championship. This was the first time a World New Vogue event was held in this country. We never doubted our studio's success. We had the talent and the teachers to prove it. Stefano Olivieri later opened a lovely dance studio in Sydney.

Other successful couples of ours were John Byrnes and Kim Fraser, John Byrnes and Kim Smith, Mark Sullivan and Debbie Gillard, Myles West and Leeanne Bampton.

Kim Fraser danced with John and had a very successful partnership. They became Australian Champions. Kim Fraser was one of my best lady Latin dancers. She gave everything from the inside. She told the story! John Byrnes married Jane Lyttleton, continuing his success and opening a successful studio in England. Mark married Debbie Gillard and they had a wonderful career. They had great rhythm for the dance and lovely posture. Myles and Leeanne also had a great career.

The Illawarra has always produced outstanding talent with wonderful achievements. Amazing where things take you! A young man from Thirroul, John O'Connell, through his dancing, successfully ended up as Mr. Cha-Cha in Strictly Ballroom and in other productions. Glenn Keenan - another one of our dancers from Newcastle, attended N.I.D.A. and was the choreographer for the stage show of Strictly Ballroom, in 1984, before the movie. He also created the character of Scott Hastings.

Stefano Olivieri and Melanie Sears (source: Melanie Sears).

Many of these dancers are still successfully involved in dancing. Their love and passion for dance remains a significant part of their lives.

Fundamentally, the construction of the dance has not changed, but minor changes have crept in. The styling of one's choreography and the styling of one's costumes have changed with progress. I don't know, but to me, some of the ladies` dancing apparel leaves a lot to be desired. We always advised our pupils about dress sense and grooming. I think they took notice.

After our successful students achieved their goals, nationally and internationally, climbing the ladder, we then carried out our next course of achievements - examinations for the course of our students. They were all taught a higher level of technique and theory and they all achieved a significant result for their examinations to be able to then teach and adjudicate.

I am so happy to have trained 40 candidates in two decades. Some students sat for more than one exam. So nice for these fine dancers to become qualified. Like ourselves, our famous dancers practiced every day. Their achievements followed with a British and World Championship. Some of them also won European and International Championships.

International learning helps anyone who wants to improve. One English coach said that, "Reeve's trained them and we claim them." We had successful couples overseas. This was very gratifying, not only for us, but for Australia as well.

Maybe our teaching methods would not be so in depth (not so serious) if we trained a beginner couple as opposed to a more top line couple. We loved to teach interstate couples. They were so challenging with knowledge, or very little of it. They were all so happy to get the feel plus the knowledge and the knowhow of the swing, sway, rise and fall. Movement and turn, when accomplished with their basic fundamentals, became the order of the day and this became the basis of swing, sway, rise and fall theory. After taking this to the next level, they were so thrilled for the explanation - of the theory and knowledge of the supporting leg.

They kept coming and we could quickly see the improvement. One lovely couple came all the way from Switzerland for a Jive lesson with me. They were enthralled with my rhythmical action - those were their words. Our teaching tools: *knowledge and feel, movement with discipline, correct posture and shape.*

Whether it be teaching an advanced competitor, a medalist or a beginner couple, I have the same approach. Teach them with confidence, humility and understanding. Make sure you are right and then do it, always! I try to make the pupil feel good. Some teachers only talk about themselves in a lesson, I don't know why.

When I am teaching, I am doing something that I love. Teaching is a passion and one which both Ray and I never forgot. In fact, at 83, I am still asked to take a lesson and that is nothing unusual. I loved my teaching and I loved showing and teaching my students. I loved to teach any pupils who wanted to learn. Some of my students and I are still in close contact. These were champions that Ray and I produced.

Some words of wisdom for any student. The pain you feel today will be the strength you feel tomorrow. Always remember that the best is yet to come, and that your current situation is not your final destination.

Your eyes are the windows to your soul - not your age.

I am a great believer that people's eyes say a lot about them.

Roll of Honour: Amateur and professional

- **JOHN & CAROL KIMMINS:** Australian Amateur Modern Champions, British Champions,, Australian Professional Champions.
- **GREG SMITH & MARION ALLEYNE:** Australian & British Amateur Modern Champions, World Amateur Modern Champions, World Amateur Latin Finalists.
- **GREG SMITH & ROSALYN TOULMIN:** Australian Amateur Latin Champions.
- **KERRY WILSON & ANN HARDING:** South Pacific, Australasian, Australian Amateur Modern & Latin Champions, Australian Professional Modern & Latin Champions, Asian Pacific Professional Modern Champions, Professional British Modern Semi Finalists & Finalists in the Quickstep.
- **KERRY WILSON & MAUREEN WILSON:** World Amateur Modern Grand Finalists.
- **KERRY WILSON & KERRY WALKER:** World Professional Modern Grand Finalists Berlin, Australian Professional Champions.
- **JOHN & WENDY THORNTON:** South Pacific, Australian & Australasian Modern Champions, British Modern Finalists.
- **DOUGLAS NEWTON & ROSALYN TOULMIN:** World Amateur Latin Grand Finalists.
- **DOUGLAS NEWTON & CANDY LANE:** 3 Time Australian Professional Latin Champions, A.D.B

Professional Ballroom and Latin Champions, Australian Reps to the World`s Professional Championships, 2 Time Queens Silver Jubilee Medal 10 Dance Professional Champions.

Doug Potter and Sue Potter.

Peter and Rosalyn Smith.

- ***JOHN BYRNES & KIM FRASER:*** South Pacific, Australian Amateur Champions Modern & New Vogue.
- ***PHILLIP LOGAN & NORMA LEE:*** Australian Amateur Latin Champions.

- ***ROBERT McKAY & VIRGINIA CHESHER:*** Australian Amateur Latin Champions.
- ***MARK & DEBBIE SULLIVAN:*** South Pacific Champions Amateur Latin, Australasian Champions Amateur Modern, East of England Professional Championships Grand Finalists.
- ***DONALD WOOD & MERILYN ROYALL:*** NSW Amateur Modern & Latin Champions, South Pacific Professional Modern, Latin Champions & New Vogue Champions.
- ***MYLES WEST & LEEANNE BAMPTON***: South Pacific Professional Champions Latin.
- ***CRAIG WILSON & LEEANNE BAMPTON:*** World Professional 10 Dance Grand Finalists, 2 Time South Pacific Professional Champions Modern.
- ***DOUG & SUE POTTER:*** Australian & Australasian Modern Professional Champions, World Championship Representatives Modern.
- ***STEFANO OLIVIERI & ANTONELLA ZUCCO:*** Junior & Youth Amateur Modern and Latin Champions.
- ***STEFANO OLIVIERI & KARINA SCHEMBRI:*** Australian Amateur Modern & Latin Champions.
- ***STEFANO OLIVIERI & MELANIE SEARS:*** World W.D.S.F. New Vogue Champions.
- ***RAY & SUE McMAHON:*** NSW State Champions Amateur and Professional, Australian Rising Star Professional Modern & New Vogue Champions.
- ***GRAHAM WILSON & DEBBIE GILLARD:*** British Junior Supporting Quickstep Competition Winners.
- ***GRAHAM WILSON & CAROLINE PAIDASCH***: South Pacific, Australasian, Australian Junior & Youth Champions Modern & Latin.

Alex Schembri and Julie Schembri (source: Alex Schembri).

- **GRAHAM WILSON & SONIA KRUGER:** Australian Professional Rising Star Champions 3 Styles.
- **IAN & MELINDA HAYES:** Australian Professional Rising Star Champions Modern.
- **KEN & JOAN MILLER:** New Zealand Amateur Modern Champions.

- ***PETER SMITH & WENDY SMITH:*** New Zealand Amateur Champions Modern & Latin.
- ***PETER SMITH & ROSALYN SMITH:*** South Pacific Professional Champions Modern.
- ***PETER & DEBBIE TODD:*** 3 Time Australian New Vogue Champions, South Pacific, Australasian Champions Modern, Latin & New Vogue Combined 8 times.
- ***ALEX & JULIE SCHEMBRI:*** Australian Modern and Latin Professional Champions, Representatives to the World Professional Modern Championships, Winners of the Invitation World Cup event, 2 Time South Pacific Professional Champions Modern & Latin.
- ***DAVID SMITH & HANNAH McCLELLAN:*** NSW Professional Modern Champions, British Closed Championship Finalists, Top 48 British Open Championships
- ***FELIX PARK & CHRISTINA PARK:*** Australian National & Australian Open, New Zealand Open, NSW Open and Asian Pacific International Amateur champions, Australian National, New Zealand Open & NSW Open Professional Champions.

The couples that are featured here in the Roll of Honour were our elite couples we trained. They won National and International titles. We also trained many other adult couples who won graded finals and championships and that were successful in their respective competitions. There were many!

We also wish to sincerely acknowledge our Juvenile and Junior couples. These youngsters won an incredible number of titles, are too numerous to mention. It is without a doubt that their contribution was just as important for the success of our studio.

David Smith and Hanna McClellan (source: David Smith).

Felix Park and Christina Park (source: Felix Park).

Never give up, no matter how you feel.

Get up, dress up, show up

And - never give up.

Donna

Someone in their egotistical manner once said that Alan and Donna had done nothing for our dancing history, though statistics beg to differ. Well, I have always said that egotism is the anesthetic of stupidity, because if they haven't, who the hell has! They have been great ambassadors for Australia and England and I as a coach and as a mother, am very proud of my daughter Donna and her husband Alan.

As I start, I put the spotlight on Donna. As a child, she was vivacious. During the 70s, children were watching Sesame Street. The show was so good for little ones learning all their letters and figures. Donna was captivated by the figure 8, which was drawn on the T.V screen. So, her father being asleep seemed to be a good target. She got out her paintbrush and painted a figure 8 on Ray's bald head. She had a lovely time and he was *non compos mentis*.

As a young girl, she was always dancing. We had some videos of dancers from overseas and Donna would watch them over and over again. I am surprised that they didn't break! Adam used to come up the backstairs after school and shout out, "not those bloody videos again".

Donna was a superb swimmer, a school champion and with not much preparation - such a talent! Donna played sports at school, but upon leaving, she concentrated on her dancing.

Donna has won many Championships, including the South Pacific, Australasian and The Australian Championships, from Juvenile, under 13 years to Adult Amateur to Professional. Her partners were Chris Brown and Paul Wilson. With Chris Brown, as a Juvenile and Junior couple, they won various Championships, including the South Pacific and Australasian. They also won at the

Australian Championships for three consecutive years. With Paul Wilson, they were a very successful Junior couple winning the South Pacific, Australasian and Asian Pacific. They also won at the Australian Championships in all three styles. Once out of the Junior ranks, Donna and Paul continued with their partnership strongly. They competed in the British Youth Latin and came 2nd and in the British Youth Modern they came third. They also represented Australia at The World Championships in Finland. As Adult Amateurs they came 10th in their first World Championship competition, and 7th in their second World Championship.

Then, at 19 years of age, Donna went to England and formed a new partnership with Claus Jordan. While representing Denmark, Donna and Claus made the semifinal of the British Open to the World Amateur Modern. They would go on to win the Australian Open Amateur Modern two years in a row.

In 1992, Donna partnered with Alan Shingler as an Amateur couple and in 1994 they were married. Between them, they made an impressive 30 British Open Finals and together made 13 International Championship, 9 United Kingdom Finals and 10 World Finals. Their success speaks for itself.

In 1998, they won the British Open to the World Amateur Modern Championships. The British Open being the title of all titles. Donna and Alan also won the International Amateur Modern Championships at Albert Hall. As Professionals they were finalists in the International for five years.

In 1999, they won the British Rising Star Open to the World Professional Modern Championships and in December of the same year they won the Professional title at the Australian Championships.

The following year they made the Grand Final of the British Open to the World Professional Championships and during that time span they won the British Closed Professional Championships.

Paul Wilson and Donna Reeve.

By now, they were rated amongst the top six professional couples internationally. They then graced the finals of all major Professional Championships. Hundreds of couples from around the world compete in these events. Donna and Alan retired in 2005 after representing England at the British Championships in the Teams Match.

Donna and Alan were honoured with the Carl Alan Award, which is presented annually in the United Kingdom honouring those who have made significant contributions to the dance industry. As Professional dancers they have taught, lectured and demonstrated in countless countries around the world!

At the Closed British Championships (a competition open only to couples representing England) a strange thing happened. When asked how they went in the British National Championships, Alan answered, "We were knocked out in the first round, literally!"

When one thinks of the quote of, "If you fail to prepare, then prepare to fail", the following is so true. I have never seen a couple like Alan and Donna prepare and train like they did for the British Championships at the Winter Gardens Ballroom in Blackpool. Donna was very aware of her diet, fitness, determination and the one thing I thought was the icing on the cake was her practice - at midnight. The reason? That was going to be the time of their Blackpool final. A strategy so well thought out.

The Good Morning Britain (G.M.B.) television show got wind of their preparation and got onto the story. Cameras followed them right up to the finals and captured their win. Asking about their preparation was one question the T.V. show asked them.

When the results came in for the British, Adam phoned us at the same time. The announcer said, "… and the winners are from the United Kingdom, Alan and Donna Shingler." Ray and I were in the lounge room and burst into tears of joy. We just couldn't help it. They did it! Donna's motto from me to her was, "never give up."

Every year we went to the British Championships to support our children and pupils. Alan and Donna had danced at The British three years prior to winning the title. In our opinion, they should have won it then. In 1998, we decided not to go, so their focus could be on preparation and not on us. Their preparation was so positive.

Alan Shingler and Donna Shingler.

Donna and Alan were invited to Elton John's birthday to dance. Elton loves ballroom dancing. They were also in the movie ENTRAPMENT, starring Catherine Zeta Jones and Sean Connery. They also appeared in the Japanese film version of the movie SHALL WE DANCE. Alan and Donna's win at the British was also mentioned in the English crime series drama LEWIS, as a question from a quiz master.

A beautiful thing that was written in the Australian Dancing Review by the editor Barry Wall. It pertained to Donna and Australia. He wrote, "the drought has broken." Not bad for a child who started dancing at minus 6 months and gave a solo demonstration on the stage at the famous Raffles Hotel, at 20 months.

Another lovely mention that was written in the January 2003 edition of the Australian Dance Review:

The floor show by Alan and Donna Shingler was nothing short of magic. They entertained and entranced the audience with some quality ballroom dancing that showed why they are one of the leading couples in this style, in the world.

We are sure when Donna danced her first Australian when she was 8 years old, she never dreamt that she would reach the stars she has. Her parents, Ray and Margaret Reeve must have been bursting with pride on Sunday night. What more could you ask for: your daughter selected as the international demonstration couple for the 60th anniversary year, topped off with your son winning both styles he competed in, in the professional ranks.

Donna and Adam would not be the dancers they are without the love and guidance they obviously received from their parents. So, we would like to congratulate not just Adam and Donna along with their respective partners, Alan and Karen but Ray & Margaret Reeve. Their first-time teachers and parents.

Australia is so lucky to have had Alan and Donna come home to impart their knowledge on Australian and International elite couples. Students have moved to our area to live, coming from - Perth, Melbourne, Brisbane, as well as overseas. Students who now call

Alan Shingler and Donna Shingler.

Australia home. One can see the improvement of those couples. All from their hard work and how they have been taught. Alan and

Donna's teaching has been so successful and rewarding. They now teach and adjudicate all over the world.

Donna was just determined from the start. Hearing it mentioned almost daily in our business, The British Championships - The Mecca of Ballroom Dancing! Donna, at around 5 years, began uttering the words, "I am going to be a British Champion," and she is! Freyja, her daughter and my granddaughter, said the same thing, only that she would be the Modern Champion and her cousin Briet from Iceland, who is Adam's daughter, could be the British Latin Champion. However, Briet has successfully gone into ballet. Soley, Adam's youngest, has become a Ballroom Dancer and together with her partner has successfully competed in the Under 12's category at The British Championships. Soley is 8 years of age. My grandson Charley, Donna's son, is a great soccer player and Freyja could be a champion at anything she does. I love them all so much, just like any grandmother. They are my life!

DONNA, what does it mean? Well, it means LADY. She is my daughter and my lady. I could not love her any more. A good person with a heart of gold. She and Alan complement each other. I do not know what I would do without her. A good mother and awesome daughter. A very successful champion dancer who gives every knowledgeable moment in what she believes and what she teaches. Donna had a dream and she fulfilled it! Never doubt yourself.

Don't worry about results

good or bad, just try and be

the best dancer you can.

I always had a dream!

Donna Reeve

Adam

Those times when Adam came up the backstairs complaining that Donna was watching those dancing videos again, little did he know that one day he would be on them, winning a championship. Everything he did was worth it.

Adam was such a great entertainer, even from an early age. Caroline Paidasch, one of our champions, was and still is a beautiful-looking girl. He asked Caroline if he could put her in the deep freeze, "What on earth for?" was her reply. "So, I can marry you when I grow up and then we will be the same age." He just loved her.

One time, when Adam was about five years old, Ray took him to the hairdresser's and Adam began to cry. He didn't want a haircut like Ray's as Ray had lost most of his hair early in life and Adam thought that his hair cut would look just like his father's.

Our friend Ray Rivers had always been a wonderful mentor and, knowing Adam's talent, asked him one day if he preferred to soar with eagles or stay with the turkeys. I think we know what Adam decided and he never looked back. When Adam was about seven years old, our family went on a holiday to Surfers Paradise, Queensland. We were invited by Ray and Robbie Rivers to stay with them. We were out to lunch at a beer garden when Adam went for a walk and he came across a cockatoo in the trees. So right away, a lovely friendship started. Adam said, "Hello Cocky", and the cocky answered "Hello Adam." Adam then proceeded to tell the cocky all about our holiday with much interest by all.

When Ray Rivers promoted his Championships at The Chevron Hilton, our families, belonging to the 3 R's, used to play under the counter lever stage. We used to take the pillows out of our rooms in case the children fell asleep. They were all such great friends.

Adam Reeve and Melinda Wall.

Adam Reeve and Louise Garvie.

As well as being a great dancer, Adam was a very good sportsman. He played soccer and cricket. Sport never eluded him. Adam also loved to surf. In the morning he would wake up, look at the beach through his bedroom window and say, "Surf's up" and away he would go with his surfboard.

Adam Reeve and Karen Reeve.

Adam was and still is, I hope, very good at impersonating people and events. His impersonation of the Indianapolis 500 car race was superb. The only thing was, he used to get into trouble with the teachers at school. In year 12, Adam starred in his high school production of West Side Story, where he played the lead character of Tony. It was a great hit in the Illawarra area.

Adam, like Donna, came through a career of success. Australian Champion in every division Juvenile, Junior and Amateur. Professional Modern and Latin European Champion. Professional World & European 10 Dance Champion, Australian and International Adjudicator.

Adam, at 8 years, was competing with Samantha Hutchison in New Zealand, at the South Pacific Juvenile Under 13 Championship, which incidentally they won. Prior to the event, the local T.V. the station did an interview with Adam and asked him why he started dancing. He said that he started dancing because his sister Donna did and his dad said that he would learn another trade. So cute from an 8-year-old.

Adam as a Junior danced at the British Championships. Years later, he would judge this very event. He was so proud of his achievements. He is still friends with many of the competitors he met on his first trip. I think by today's efforts, the camaraderie isn't the same as it was back then.

Adam won with his various partners at the South Pacific, Australasian and the Australian Championships. Starting out his career with Samantha Hutchison from NSW, as a Juvenile and Junior competitor. His other partners were - Stacey Geyer (Queensland), Kelly Barratt-Thompson (NSW), Kelly Newton (Victoria), Rebecca Allen (Perth), Louise Garvie (Scotland), Melinda Wall (NSW) and Karen Byjork-Reeve (Iceland). His major wins were with Samantha Hutchison, Rebecca Allen, Melinda Wall, Louise Garvie and Karen Reeve.

As far as competitive alertness, Adam used to say, "It'll be right on the day." Bob Courts - God rest his soul, said "Hell, what do you feed Adam on?" I would always reply, "High Octane."

At the Asian Pacific Amateur Championships in Tokyo, Japan, Adam had to give a speech on behalf of Australia. He gave it in Japanese! The dancing fraternity in Japan was so excited because of this. He would return some years later with Karen winning the World Professional 10 Dance Championships.

Adam has done some wonderful things. He and Louise Garvie did an ad on T.V for *Lift* soft drink in Bournemouth, UK. They did it at night time in a water fountain. It must have been freezing. As part of the original cast of BURN THE FLOOR, Adam and Karen appeared on Broadway, Radio City. It was so exciting and people were dancing in the aisles during the show. Such a tremendous success and it affected them so. The show went all around the world and continues to have worldwide acclaim. Adam also made a short movie for a film festival. The movie was called THE AUSTRALIAN. Adam played a gangster who was a wanted man. In the movie there was a couple who did the Tango, all part of Adam's choreography. Being the director, it showed more of his creativity. Adam is regularly called upon as the creative director and choreographer for Iceland's DANCING WITH THE STARS.

Adam has had lovely and successful dance partners who all achieved in their own right. I told him not to worry, that he would find the right partner in the end and he did. Adam went to England to improve his study and international experience. In 1997, whilst in England, he met Karen and formed a partnership in 1998. In 2001, they got married.

I told Adam, when he went to England, to only go to the best teachers - those who have achieved themselves and taught pupils who have done the same. *You can't take anyone there, if you haven't been there yourself.* Very true! I know if I was competing in this era, I would want to go to a coach who has been there, done it and has the right information. Don't waste your money on someone who makes out they know something but have produced no one or done anything. They just trade off someone else's teaching - a very flimsy future in my book.

Adam Reeve and Karen Reeve.

I think at the time, the Australian administration was ignorant not to have helped and sponsor Adam and Karen to represent Australia. Iceland (being Karen's homeland) took the opportunity to sponsor them to represent at the World Professional 10 Dance Championships. It was great for Iceland, as Adam and Karen won. Iceland's first and only World Championship winners!

Iceland rejoiced for the win. Australia, for their bad foresight, missed out. Adam remains the only Australian to win a World Professional 10 Dance Championship. My beloved country needs much help in administration indeed.

Adam and Karen Reeve - Australian, Icelandic, European Champions 2000 - 2003. World 10 Dance Professional Champions 2003. World and British adjudicators.

Adam's question as a young man was, "Why can't everyone be nice?" My son-in-law Alan's question years later was, "Why can't the people in our industry be honest?" Touché!

Believe in yourself and your vision.

Now be nice!

Adam Reeve

Ray

Ray Reeve.

RAYMOND HENRY REEVE: husband, father, grandfather, competition champion, trainer of champions and always passionate about his dancing. He was also a very private person. Ray always applauded good dancing, and if anyone asked him, he was always honest with his answer, in his mind.

From buying a small truck in the morning for 10 pounds and selling it in the afternoon for 20. To somersaulting over the handlebars on Adam's Honda bike on our reserve. To help put out the bushfires on our property in 1968, or just giving a dance lesson - it was all just part of life. It was who he was.

One instance, whilst representing the S.A.T.D. in New Zealand at The Australasian, the teams had been booked by the organisers into a temperance hotel (meaning no alcohol). However, when young people are celebrating their wins, they have a party, and so did our dancers. In the morning, Peter Todd asked, "What will we do with the empty bottles?" Ray said, "Don't worry, I will attend to it", and he did. He put them outside the girl's door. He had a good sense of humour. Not so much when he got older, but uncomplicated and easy to live with.

The dancing fraternity called him THE LITTLE KING. His initials spoke for themselves, R.H.R. Our colleagues thought it was great.

When it came to teaching, he never altered his method. In fact, Ray taught a lovely young lady, Janet Ware, who was partially blind. He convinced Janet to go for her Solo Statuette at the I.D.M.A. Championships, the highest medal in the I.D.M.A Association, an English Association. He instructed her just the same as he did any other student and as if no one knew of her incapacity.

When he taught beginners, Ray's most important rule was to teach everyone the forward and backward walk, which was a basic balancing exercise. This also incorporated the timing of each step, which was a two-beat slow on each step, so it was counted 1, 2, 3, 4, which was a bar of music in Foxtrot time.

Timing and Rhythm were so important, which was cultivated by learning the theory and technique of the dance. After all, that's what we did - dance to the rhythm and timing of a particular dance.

Ray would always analyse his students and he was very good at it. Though the thing that most annoyed Ray about pupils was laziness in their practice. Hence the quote Fail to prepare, then prepare to fail`.

As a competitive couple, we trained a lot. My brothers thought our fitness was the same as their football training, the way we were running around the dance floor. We weren't a good team; we were a great team! Both of us attended to what we had to do. During our competitive years and towards the end, for Ray, dancing grew a bit thin with the introduction of people who were not as dedicated as we had known. Quality and honesty were losing their importance.

Ray never slackened off with this teaching. Every lesson he gave 100%. The timing of us representing Australia and dancing in Europe with a revolution in choreography that was introduced to the world was an exciting time. With the strength of overseas dancing, and to have had the opportunity to be a part of that, was a pivotal moment in our dancing careers. We were truly inspired.

After we came back from overseas in 1965, we headed to New Zealand to compete, teach and lecture. With our teaching, our emphasis was to focus on the basics - we felt that this was paramount. Also, I was insistent upon it. We focused on the basic waltz. Both of us thought it was lacking, but with good basic training, it would improve their dancing quickly, allowing them to move forward with their understanding and ability. We left New Zealand and came back the next year to run our lectures and teach again. To our dismay, the dancing hadn't improved. In fact, it had taken a step back. Everyone seemed to just want to learn new choreography. It was quite disappointing. I am a firm believer that if you can't perform the basics well, how can you perform extended choreography any better?

Luckily, there were a few teachers who understood where we were coming from and together, we were able to convince them of the importance of basic training. As we travelled to New Zealand over the coming years, the students worked really hard and became lovely dancers. They were well trained, and one could see the vast improvement.

Ray never read many books. He was a visual learner. I pushed Ray to get his teaching degree. At first, he was a bit reluctant. So, I went over the theory with him every day for six weeks. I ended up doing my degree as well. Ray would become quite the teacher.

With Ray's consistency in good teaching, he won the Brolga Award for the best teacher of the year. He won this award eight years in a row! Quite the feat indeed. After that time, they changed the rules. Perhaps it was because he won *too many*.

Another note of his foxtrot, which was also his initials R. R. which was the Rolls Royce action. His peers gave this term to Ray, because they felt his foxtrot was smooth, classic, just like the car itself. Ray loved teaching and dancing but didn't like practice. Before every show, we would pop into the studio and go through our routines. We thought it was a good idea. As a bit of fun, before each competition, I would write my name in Ray's lesson book if he had a space. We did everything together.

Ray also received awards for being accepted into the Hall of Fame and the Hall of Legions. The board of control selected these awards. Receiving these awards required sound credentials as an Australian and International adjudicator. In 1971, Ray had judged the World Championships in Berlin & Korea and also the International Ballroom Championships at the Royal Albert Hall in London. Both events were held in the same year.

Ray officially retired from teaching in 1996. I carried on with teaching for the next six years. Ray seemed a little disappointed in the way students seemed to just want the instant results. There never seemed to be a long-term goal. No one wanted to put in months, or even years, of hard work to get the results that they were looking for. It had to be now. Totally different to how we approached our dancing. When we were told by Tess Sculley, to go home and practice for five years. We were taken aback, but boy was she correct! Five years later, we were unstoppable.

In the end, Ray couldn't have been prouder of his students and especially his children and the dancers that they had become. When Donna won the British with Alan, and Adam won the World's with Karen - it was such a moment for him and for us. There was no doubt in Ray's mind that his children were going to be world class dancers, no doubt. It was his dream as much as it was theirs!

Take a step and stand on it.

Measure!

Ray Reeve

Leaving a legacy

As part of the lead up to the 1984 Asian Pacific, which was held in Sydney, at the Entertainment Centre, the media coverage was great. The A.B.C. selected to televise a show about how successful our studio was. The main story centred on Donna and Paul's career as part of the introduction. The tape showed all of our other successful students as well.

Donna and Paul were the Junior Champions at the time. The story followed their success right up to the championships and during the wonderful footage. The cameraman was so unique. He filmed the whole take on roller skates. We were all mesmerised. It was said his camera cost $30,000 dollars. He was magical.

Starting from the studio through to the Entertainment Centre, they filmed and interviewed many during the championships. At the end, as a backdrop for the credits, they used Donna and Paul's competition as they stood on the dais as winners. Their names were on the credits, too. Adam and Samantha were also on the footage for the Juvenile Championships. This was a beautiful memory.

Fast forward to my Junior daughter and my Juvenile son, now helping to coordinate the most fantastic Oz Dance Camp. Who would have thought? The Oz Dance Camp was held in Wollongong in 2003. Alan, Donna, Adam and Karen were the organisers. They invited the World's top coaches in Modern and Latin to lecture and to coach dancers from all over Australia, Japan, South Korea, Taiwan, England, Iceland and New Zealand.

Alan and Donna taught in one room, Adam and Karen in another, and our guest teachers taught in yet another. Practice times were arranged for the couples along with lectures. This spectacular event was held at Wollongong's premier hotel, the Novotel. All the visiting teachers, couples and dance lovers stayed at the hotel.

I walked up the beautiful staircase to the first floor. Everything was so busy and exciting. Stalls with loads of dancing attire and music. The sellers were readily available for people to peruse and buy.

The night-time programme was a ball, during which our audience was entertained by magnificent exhibitions, being performed by magnificent Ballroom and Latin Couples from all over Australia.

Also, we celebrated our studio's 50th year of operation. We received a beautiful letter from the then prime minister John Howard. It was all so exciting.

The Oz Dance Camp ran for 4 years and I must say it was the most fantastic promotion that I have ever seen and have ever been to. To promote the Oz Dance Camp, Adam and Karen taught Salsa on the beach at North Wollongong, opposite the Novatel during the day on the Saturday and Sunday before the beginning of the lectures and lessons. Hundreds attended the well organised Salsa class and it was for free! I think this was the first time Salsa was taught on the beach. What a wonderful opportunity for everyone to achieve such a wealth of knowledge. There has never been such a promotion. All had a great time. Organised by my FAB 4. The most electrifying extravaganza I have ever attended and all in Wollongong, home to the Illawarra.

The Illawarra area has always been strongly competitive in swimming, basketball, tennis, cricket and ballroom dancing. In the Illawarra, it has long been considered that Ballroom Dancing has won more championships on a whole than any other sport. Hence the dance studios that sprung up everywhere to make it possible for people to learn to dance.

The Fab Four (Donna, Adam, Karen and Alan).

Personally, I am very proud of the quote from one of our colleagues who said our studio was the best and most successful studio in Australia, possibly in the world. We were not the first or the only studio locally. Each and every one of the following people contributed to the development of Ballroom Dancing in the area, in one way or another. These are the names of the teachers and places of tuition. Wally Madigan - Thirroul, Dick and Dulcie Johns - Wollongong, Lloyd and Beverly Saunders - Unanderra, Neville and Helen Smith - Mt Ousley, Wollongong and Gordon and Margaret Reeve Wallace - Nowra.

Max and Dawn Wright were a young married couple who learnt from Ray and I, and they too were talented dancers. They taught at the Illawarra Yacht Club and contributed to the teaching of competitive couples, who we were privileged to teach.

Then we have Jim and Jean Davey. Jim and Jean migrated to Australia in the sixties, from Scotland. For a short while, they lived at the hostel at Fairy Meadow. They then bought a house at Russell Vale. They were talented dancers and at the time we always chose them to dance the Tango in our team whenever representing our studio. As well as lovely dancers, they were also well-educated in the technique and presentation of the dance. Studying very well for their professional examinations with me. They were highly commended.

They then started teaching at the Fraternity Bowling Club, in Fairy Meadow, very successfully for many years. Unfortunately, when studying for their Fellowship, which is the highest technique award, Jim became very ill and went to hospital. He never came home. We enjoyed their company and respect. When I would come out of the Latin room after taking them for a theory lesson, I would take off Jim with his Scottish accent (always with affection) saying: "Slaw, slaw, quick, quick, slaw." True friends and good Professionals.

And then `The Reeve Academy of Ballroom Dancing`, Thirroul and Woonona - Ray and Margaret Reeve, now Dancespace 383, a continuation of our studio. We retired and then Alan and Donna, along with Adam and Karen, took over at the helm very successfully. They are now invited all over the world to teach, lecture and demonstrate. Adam and Karen, after a short while, decided to go back to Karen's homeland, Iceland, to live. They taught and have now cemented an excellent dancing structure in Iceland and are very well known there.

Alan and Donna continued with Dancespace 383. They moved to Wollongong and kept up their competitive couples, hosting many international visitors for lessons.

When you look back at the studios that emerged in Sydney, there are some stand out names: Segars Ballroom, Phyllis Bates, Jack Keating, Froulop and Paton, The Penelope Cay School of Dancing, Joan Allen, Miss Misdale Studio and Jimmy Anderson.

People from everywhere would go dancing and that's when the teaching came into vogue. The teachers became qualified to teach and improved the standard in the way of medal tests and social dancing. Then competitive dancing raised its head.

The social dances were held at Surreyville, Marrickville, The Strollers and the Albert Palais in Leichhardt, in their dance halls and their studios. These were all advertised in the newspaper.

I can remember my parents going to Tea Gardens on Sydney Harbour on a Sunday in the summer. Swim all day and dance all night. Of course, this was much earlier than the establishment of studios. It has been noted that in life generally, one would like to be able to sing or dance. Also seen in the American dance halls and the English ballroom dancing halls, including the afternoon tea dances at the Cafe De (Paris) pronounced Paree. People just loved to dance to the new rhythms created.

American Swing and the English Quickstep's music changed. It seemed to be a bit shallow in the offering. Then, just like Glen Miller, who was searching for a sound, the sounds of the bands became wholesome. Benny Goodman, Artie Shaw, Duke Ellington, Count Basie and Woody Herman created such great sounds. These were the times that I grew up in. The Negro American music had the best rhythm. It made you feel like dancing. Lindy Hop, Jive, Jitterbug and the free flow of dance.

The great singers of the day joined these bands. It was just a smorgasbord of rhythm and blues. I don't think we have had in this arena, singers like those ladies of that era. Ella Fitzgerald, Sarah Vaughan, Lena Horne, Etta James, Nina Simone, Aretha Franklin and Dinah Washington. I could go on and on. The lady singers of that era gave the singers of today their shoulders to stand on and learn. I don't think that we can ramble off *all* those wonderful pioneers, as there were so many of them.

The English bands came back into the loop for composing rhythms for Ballroom Dancing. Hence, the English Waltz - Joe Loss, Victor Silvester and Ken Mackintosh all catered to one's need to dance to the strict ballroom rhythms.

This is just an overall observation. The ballroom competitive scene came of age. The societies set up their structure and set out theory agendas for the Professionals to study and learn, to take their exams and to adjudicate. I used to love to judge in the competitions when we weren't competing.

The entire scene was a glamorous one. In fact, I used to wear a hat and short gloves to judge in the afternoon sessions and soon the other lady adjudicators did the same. Shoes and handbag to match. No slacks either. We all wore dresses or skirts and definitely no track suits for the successful competitors to be presented with their prizes. And yes, I agree with this statement, as of today. The male spectators wore suits.

Things have changed a lot since I started dancing - not always for the best. With all things I have always thought, don't find fault, fix it! I just hope that our next generation of dancing has a time of enjoyment and learning, as I did and still do. So much knowledge to gain, while much was appreciated.

When dancing was at its peak, Ray and I were involved with and taught the principles of every major studio in Sydney. We made a great impact on the dancing scene all over Australia and New Zealand. It is very hard to express the lovely emotions. We felt so good and content in our life. Ray and I weren't a good team, we were a great team. I would not change anything.

Having made my own dresses, including dresses for the girls in the studio, it all became too much. So, I ended up going to Judy Wade's mother, Nola Lowe and Dolly Strowbridge. Nola Lowe really carried on for many years for lots of competitors. These women were great dressmakers.

My gorgeous family.

I aimed for two dresses a year and sometimes ended up with three. Grooming and deportment were so important to me. Each Saturday of the competitions, I went to the hairdressers. I couldn't do my own hair at the time, but I learnt very quickly. Ray's cousin, Patsy Nobes, used to do my hair - she was great. When I went to England, I had to learn to do my own. I also took a hair piece for emergencies.

The English girl competitors had lovely skin, and they were very interested in my make-up. I used a Max Factor pan stik and a loose powder. They used little make-up, but on the floor with the lights, one needed a bit more. You might say they were really interested. Shoes - I had to get them made and later was able to get them from London.

I danced with a local boy called André Young and we climbed through our grades. He was a great person, a wonderful dancer, with a great attitude. I felt we took our dancing to another level, but that was nothing compared to my partnership with Ray. With Ray, we did some interesting things.

Apparently, the ladies' dance dresses originally were made of chiffon and georgette, over net petticoats - not too full. These lovely materials were flowing. The petticoats were made of rayon net. When we made our petticoats out of rayon net, we would put paraffin wax on the net and iron it in place, to make it stiffer. They would take hours of ironing but later we were able to get nylon net, which didn't need ironing and was easier to sew.

If one did not have chiffon, the dancers used organdy or organza fabric and the length of the dresses were somewhat longer. Everything pertaining to deportment was so important to help the execution of one's performance. And then the dress styling changed. I thought some of the Latin dresses were risqué. That little slogan *it's better to conceal, than reveal!*

Dancing competitively, one had to present a lovely image, being a *sight act*. Everything contributed to one's success. Ray created our choreography in the Modern and myself in the Latin style. I changed my hair colour to blonde. We always created entrances for our shows and lovely endings that fitted to the music.

On our first trip to the United Kingdom, one of our coaches, the great Len Scrivener, said, "And which Australian champions are you?" Ray, very honestly answered, "We have not won an Australian Championship yet, Mr. Scrivener. We have come here to learn." Scrivener responded with, "Oh the man has a brain".

We learnt so much from him. He explained that he had taught couples who all said that they were Australian Professional Champions. Today, some of the competitive couples in Australia *think* they are World Champions. I am sure they don't fully comprehend what it takes to be a World Champion. The most important thing is that one has to be good enough. Learning about our time with Henry Jacques, Scrivener took us out to lunch just to hear the theories that Henry taught us. He agreed with his theories and then he added his own ideas, continuing with his book, JUST ONE IDEA, and joined with Henry Jacques` book, MODERN BALLROOM DANCING. A wealth of knowledge had been made available to us. Learning was at a premium.

I have witnessed in my lifetime some of the great dancing. Coming of our age, we had these great coaches. Jacques, Scrivener, Binick, and from the masters of dancing - Bill and Bobbie Irvine, Peter Eggleton and Brenda Winslade, Richard and Janet Gleave, Michael and Vicky Barr and Anthony and Fay Hurley. These great masters paved the way for the future generation and then they continued.

I call these next champions the powerhouse of execution. They had a lovely rhythm with great movements, but also a commitment to their dancing. They carried on through the legacy that they had been given by the masters. I was so lucky to see these greats as well. John Wood and Ann Gleave, Marcus and Karen Hilton, Andrew Sinkinson and Loraine Barry.

I found those couples most powerfully entertaining with great movement, line, technique, posture and correctness. They changed the excitement of Modern dancing, having their wonderful coaches to lay the foundation for them. Henry Jacques, in his words, "As the lady develops, her shape would get bigger". We have foot rhythm and body rhythm.

When it comes to Latin, there is nothing today like Donnie Burns and Gaynor Fairweather or Bryan Watson and Carmen Vincelj. They were the most rhythmical Latin dancers I have ever seen. The focus was always on rhythm and line. Beautiful to watch.

I have gone off the Latin style at the moment. There is no story between the man and the lady in the partnership. They both dance their well-executed, beautifully rehearsed routines without togetherness. All too clinical! All great dancers pursue their own right, but I feel they don't tell the story of the dance. They could do with a bit of Delroy and Dulaine in their routines.

One day Neil Rosenfeld phoned me. It was nice to hear from him. During the conversation, he told me he wished Ray and I had had more children and then Australia would have had more champions. It was such a nice comment. We keep in touch.

I recently watched the final of a great championship event and of the six grand finalists, only one couple stood out. They had the X factor. They were so lovely. The other five couples used so much physical effort in their dancing and weren't nice to watch. Hence, minimum effort for maximum effect - Henry's statement, which we totally agreed with. As he once answered a professional at a meeting, "What came first, the chicken or the egg?" "What came first, the dancer or the book?"

I have shared a wonderful life with Ray, something I would never change. A greater success I would never ask for. I have won 5 Brolga awards for the top teacher of the year. I have judged 4 World Championships plus many international events, but my biggest prize - my beautiful children! Not only as a parent, but as a teacher. Being part of their dance journey from juveniles right up into their adult careers. Teaching them was a privilege. All that matters is that they are good people with their spouses, who are good people too. They are much loved and very successful.

The same as Ray and I. I am a wife, mother, grandmother and I suppose one would say a champion dancer and a successful teacher and professional. Everything I learnt, I was taught to make sure it was right and then did it. You have to accept the positive, eliminate the negative, latch onto the superlative and don't mix with Mr. in between.

Ray and I retired from competing, winning the Captain Cook Bi-Centenary Championships in 1970. Seeing that we would not be here for the next one, we thought it would be a nice championship to finish with. We retired as the Triple Undefeated Professional Champions.

In saying so, my family and I have all judged a World Championship event. I still have a wonderful life and have looked forward to this year, 2023, when our studio will celebrate its 70th year of trading, and you're all invited! I think just about everyone on the South Coast, some time or other, has been to our studio.

Yes, dancing has given me a life of moments, but throughout it all, they were never dull. Coming back from New Zealand one year, from the South Pacific's, we flew Pan American Airlines. They gave the students such a great deal on their air fares. Donna and Adam sat together near the window. Donna was looking out the window and said, 'Mum, there is a hole in the wing." My reply was to her, "Don't be silly, you're looking at the flaps." However, I checked it out, and she was right. There was a hole in the wing.

I reported it to the hostess and she moved the three of us to other seats. I was handling the situation until the hostesses took their high-heeled shoes off. The captain made the announcement that there was a hole in the wing and that everything was okay and that he had a luncheon date in Sydney and he was positive about making it.

We were very nervous, as the hole was very big. Much to our amazement, the students played out the movie FLYING HIGH. We were all thinking the worst. The captain flew the plane home over the ocean at just 1,000 feet. He was playing it safe and we all lived to face another day. Like I said, never a dull moment. THANK GOD!

As I was writing this chapter, we were in our second year of the Covid pandemic and it felt like all hell's breaking loose. I had one of my falls and I had to go to the hospital. I could not walk and ten weeks later I was on a walker. The pain was excruciating and as I write these words, I am in Figtree Private Hospital rehabilitating. I am now being taken to Shellharbour to have an MRI. Hopefully, it will find something in my leg and I am having another one tomorrow. The specialist thinks I will need a hip operation. Good news! After three MRIs, the Doctor's report gives me hope and a bit of a smile. No fractures in the hip.

There appears to be a nerve resting on the degenerated disc, causing the worst pain I have ever imagined. My fractured ankle does not have the pain like it does in my thigh. Lucky for me, they did not have to operate on the femur. Now for the next stage of my treatment: injections and physiotherapy. I am pleased they did not have to operate.

An amazing thing happened while I was in the first hospital, Wollongong. My brother Kevin had been very ill for three years. While speaking to my sister-in-law Carmel, she mentioned ward B3 in the hospital. I very vaguely picked up the name B3 and said to her I am in B3 and she said so is your brother Kevin. I did not know that he was in the hospital. So here we were, brother and sister in the same ward, back-to-back. He was in the room next door. I asked the nurses not to tell him I was here. The next morning, I visited him and we shared some lovely time together. One could not imagine this happening in a million years. I was then transferred to Figtree Private Hospital, and they transferred Kevin to Bulli District Hospital. However, with much sadness, he passed away. His illness was too great for him to have survived.

I recovered and went home to isolate, then to top it all off, I had two more falls. I was hospitalised from February to August. There had been three deaths in my family that year. Two brothers and a sister-in-law. Leo, one of my brothers, was a front row forward and he played in the N.R.L. I think the tackles he encountered during the games weren't good for him overtime. There is a lot of information now about head high tackles.

A chapter of our life is ending. It was a lovely path we were travelling on. A great experience, with two wonderful children. I am blessed to have such a lovely life and with the highs and the lows, I wouldn't change a thing. I am so proud of my wonderful husband, my children's achievements, my wonderful grandchildren, my extended family and great friends.

My children will always be tied to me. They are the things that hold my life together. They are the light in my eyes and the beat of my heart, no matter how exhausted I am. I will always try to move mountains for them. They are very blessed to have wonderful spouses to share with their families for the rest of their lives.

When one speaks of a legacy, what can one say? To our successful children, whom I love dearly and who I am very proud of. No one knows how their children will turn out. Ray and I were lucky parents. Our children, Donna and Adam, could not have turned out any better. With love and know-how, we tried our best with encouragement and they turned out good people. They carried this into their dancing, to their teachers and competitors. Both married, one British Champion, the other a World Champion. What more could they do? We enjoyed their successes that were nurtured along the way. This legacy of love and knowledge will carry on from their parents hoping to encounter such a life. Thank you for being you!

This legacy I also leave to my pupils and the dancing fraternity. The knowledge that I have gained and the enjoyment of learning and understanding my chosen profession. It (my life) has been a lifetime of endearment and love. My teaching and the wonderful people I have taught, met and introduced to dancing. For sixty years, I never stopped learning, hoping this knowledge lives on forever. This I leave to you.

My life was and still is of giving, by whatever means, of establishing our successful career. Tributes and acknowledgements received made me feel appreciated. Now, at 84 years, I still give theory lessons and prepare people for their Professional Exams. I love to watch the wonderful students in their practice class at Dancespace. The pupils are very friendly and respectful. I am so content, to say the least.

If I had my way, I would like to see all our teachers in the industry start their pupils and teach classes from the ground roots, as we all did in the past.

Some great champions came from these routine intrinsic values, and I would love to see the teaching to pupils of the basic amalgamations instead of going straight into fancy variations. It is a wonderful thing to learn to dance. Knowing what to do in a basic structure, makes it easier to learn.

Now that I have come to the end of my book, I can't stop thinking about what a wonderful time I have experienced. I sincerely hope you have enjoyed the read. And as for me? *It's Back to the Ballroom.*

Life's not about standing around waiting

for the storm to pass.

It's about learning how to dance in the rain!

Printed by Libri Plureos GmbH in Hamburg, Germany